For Your Displeasure Plays (Volume One)

Alan Pickthall

Copyright © 2015 Alan Pickthall

All rights reserved.

ISBN:1508808562
ISBN-13:9781508808565

CONTENTS

	Acknowledgments	i
1	Four Farmers	1
2	That Creeper Man Dance	32
3	Insomniac Clowns	48
4	The Leather Dinner Party	81
5	Crow's Feet	113
6	Cade Relief and His Butter Feet	131
7	Clyde^2 = Auntie Lydia	142

ACKNOWLEDGMENTS

Thank you to all the actors involved in performances of *For Your Displeasure* plays since 2007.

Four Farmers

Written by Alan Pickthall 2014

Characters

James *(a farmer)*

Bob *(a farmer)*

Hector *(a farmer)*

Timothy *(an apprentice)*

THE 1ST SCENE OF THE PLAY CALLED FOUR FARMERS

We are in the living room of a farmhouse, where four wooden chairs stand across the centre of the floor. There is a small table separating them. There is a big window at the back of the stage.

BOB, a farmer sits on the first of the chairs next to JAMES, another farmer who has an empty chair to his left. They both hold cups.

JAMES: How are the pigs?

BOB: Oh, very plump. How's the sheep?

JAMES: Woolly, so very woolly. I did notice, the other day, one particular pig with the juiciest behind I've seen for a long time.

BOB: You mean Barry?

JAMES: Do I?

BOB: Well-built, friendly, nice round arse?

JAMES: That's right.

BOB: That's Barry that is.

JAMES: He's a good one alright. Wouldn't mind a piece of that arse me!

BOB: A scrumptious arse… a bit of a salt, dollop of brown.

JAMES: You could have butties for a week with an arse like that. Could I maybe put my name down for a bit of Barry?

BOB considers this for a second.

BOB: Now, see here.

JAMES: I'm seeing Bob, I'm seeing.

BOB: The thing is, though my tummy rumbles and my lips lick themselves with little lip-tongues when looking at that pert pair of piggy buttocks…

JAMES: You've gone and bloody done it haven't you?

BOB: I haven't finished, being fair.

JAMES: Grown fond of Barry haven't you? Like a pet now, is he? Can't bring yourself to slap those buns between good, sliced sesame?

BOB: *(Drops head)* Aye, you speak true James. I'm afraid you've said exactly how I feel. You have put my feelings into words and told me them back.

BOB reaches out for a biscuit and takes one.

BOB: Biscuits don't have feelings do they? They don't look at you with big eyes! You dunk, dip if it's a Rich-Tea, and then gulp, gone! A fleeting relationship that is… Barry is different.

JAMES: Livestock Bob, Barry is live… *stock!* Think of them as part of the family and you're knee-deep in dung with no money in your pocket, and a Christmas card list the opposite size to Everest!

BOB: Everest's a big bastard!

JAMES: It is indeed Bob, bloody huge is that. Kill it, cook it, eat it, that's all I'm saying on the matter.

BOB: I can't put Barry through that motto James. I just can't. He understands me, he does. I say his name and he smiles at me. Have you never grown attached to a sheep before?

JAMES: Not any real ones. No tears were shed when she popped anyhow.

BOB eats his biscuit.

BOB: These biscuits taste good.

JAMES: Never been a big fan of biscuits. I like my meat.

They sip from their cups.

JAMES: I tell a lie…

BOB: Everybody likes a custard cream. I've yet to meet a farmer who doesn't nibble the odd one or twelve.

JAMES: No, I mean Sheila.

BOB: Who's Sheila?

JAMES: A sheep I had once upon a rainbow. I did find it hard saying goodbye to that one.

BOB: Was it the eyes?

JAMES: Mostly.

BOB: Windows to the soul James, that's what they are, circular windows to the soul.

JAMES: I've heard that one Bob. I've heard people say that very thing.

BOB: And you sent those big eyes to slaughter?

JAMES: I had to.

BOB: With those feelings and all?

JAMES: No, I got around that one.

BOB: Do tell.

JAMES: I'm telling. Got a mate didn't I? He sprayed bad language down each side of her coat. Now I don't abide swearing of any kind and they put me right off her, dirty bitch.

JAMES sips his tea.

BOB: Poor Sheila.

JAMES: Aye, let's have a drink to Sheila.

They both sip from their cups.

JAMES / BOB: To Sheila!

JAMES: *(Raising cup)* And here's to Barry.

BOB: To Baaa… no, not as of yet.

JAMES: We'll see.

They both drink and leaves blow in from SL where HECTOR enters. He is a bearded farmer, perhaps a little older than the others. He wears a big duffel coat and a flat cap.

HECTOR: It's blowing a gale out there gentlemen, blowing a right old gale. I think that fence will need steadying soon enough. I don't want my cows wandering down into the village, spooking folk.

JAMES: You have to be wary of fences Hector. *(To BOB)* Be aware of all fences!

BOB: *(To HECTOR)* He's right you know. It's those gales. How I hate all gales! *(To JAMES)* Yes, I know that's her name.

HECTOR: I shall have to put into action an 'action plan' for all of this bad weather we've been having.

JAMES: Couldn't agree much more Hector. Bob, do you remember that time when a gust of wind blew my trousers right down to my boots? Vicar's wife got and eyeful I tell you, I was going all kinds of commando that day!

BOB: It was unfortunate that your trousers blew down as I was turning the corner.

JAMES: It was, I tell you, oh it was.

BOB: Even more unfortunate that you didn't seem to be in any hurry to pull them back up again, from boot to belt.

JAMES: *(To HECTOR)* The damage was already done wasn't it? No point in hurrying.

BOB: Then they kept falling down didn't they?

JAMES: Damn wind, it's true! Had to keep covering myself up with a very unfortunate tugging motion! Poor Vicar's wife, poor, sexy Vicar's wife!

BOB: It was a still day if I remember. The hottest day of the year so I heard.

JAMES: Let's stop remembering now Bob, forget it ever happened.

HECTOR: It most certainly was the hottest day of the year. Bessie, my prize cow, looked like she was dancing on ice. Like that telly programme, where they dance on ice.

JAMES: That Philip Schofield talks to the screen in that one. Asks me to phone numbers for no reason.

BOB: You vote for your favourite dancing couple.

JAMES: No, there's more to it than that. He has a right dirty look in his eyes when he reads loads of zeroes.

BOB: My wife has a candle for that Schofield fella, has his face on it too. A 'silver fox' she says. I don't get that because foxes have been killing my chickens haven't they? Fancies a murderer she does.

HECTOR takes off his coat and hangs it over the back of a chair.

HECTOR: I've earned a brew I think.

He sits down next to JAMES.

HECTOR: What are you both supping?

JAMES: Tea Hector.

BOB: *Cups* of tea.

HECTOR: Don't worry Bob, I'll join you.

JAMES takes a hip flask from a trouser pocket.

JAMES: Or perhaps you'd care for something stronger?

BOB: Put that away.

JAMES: He's been out in the bitterest cold with the cows Bob. He may need a warming through.

HECTOR: I would, but I better not.

JAMES: It's your farm.

HECTOR: We're sat in my farmhouse.

JAMES: And the wife's away.

HECTOR: Enjoying a weekend of knitting.

JAMES: Then…

JAMES holds up his flask.

JAMES: Get yourself warm.

BOB reaches over and intercepts the flask.

JAMES: What's your problem?

BOB: We agreed that this would be a dry weekend.

HECTOR: Bob is right, we need clear heads so we can discuss the farmers market down in Twiddlington.

JAMES: The 'Farmers Market' will be the same as it always is, cheese and the like, let's make a night a good one.

BOB: You know better.

JAMES sips from his flask and becomes momentarily drunk.

JAMES: I haven't got eighty cans of bitter stashed in my willies Bib!

HECTOR: I rarely touch a drop nowadays anyway. Plus I've got the lad out there.

JAMES: The lad?

HECTOR: My apprentice… he's got the spare room whilst Mrs Hector is away.

JAMES: This one of those larks by the government?

BOB: *(Emotional)* The government.

HECTOR: He's a good lad, though it'll be a time before he can call himself a real farmer. You start at the bottom I suppose and his heart is centred just right.

JAMES: Does this lad have a name?

HECTOR: Aye, Timothy they call him. But I call him Timmy, saves time. He seems keen but slow on the uptake as things stand.

JAMES: Sounds like me when I wasn't yet a fully blown farmer… only a …

BOB: Farm?

JAMES: When I was only a farm yes, wait, that can't be right.

HECTOR: Shall we have a bite to eat?

JAMES: Let's order pizza.

HECTOR: Haven't any in the freezer.

JAMES: I understand, so let us order a pizza, a big one, the size of all our faces, if they were massive.

BOB: Don't be asking for those silly little slices of sausage on top.

JAMES: Pepperoni is that, a lovely sausage. I love to chew on that particular sausage. Hector, what do you favour?

HECTOR: Are we talking pizza or sausage?

JAMES: Sausage.

HECTOR: That's one of those questions I find so difficult to answer. I will tell you one that I cannot abide by… that curly, whirly one.

JAMES / BOB: Cumberland!

HECTOR: A Cumberland sausage! It's so packed tight and circular, I hate it. A right meaty vortex to hell is that sausage. When I get a tummy ache, I imagine my insides resemble a shaking Cumberland sausage.

BOB: *(Shakes head)* Nightmare image!

HECTOR: I tasted your sausage the other day Bob. That was a nice fat one. It was flavoursome and not reminiscent of my internals.

BOB: 'Twas a good sausage, from a healthy pig. That's why I keep them so well. Don't I do just that James?

JAMES: He does keep them well, doesn't he Hector?

HECTOR: Keeps them well he does.

BOB: I do keep them well.

JAMES / HECTOR: He does.

JAMES: One in particular.

BOB stands.

BOB: Leave Barry's poor arse alone!

HECTOR: Have I missed something?

JAMES: Our friend Bob here has become attached to a curly-tailed little blighter he has, goes by the name of Barry, oink!

BOB: I keep him well and all.

JAMES: I bet you ruddy well do.

BOB sits back down and JAMES stands.

JAMES: Where's the telephone Hector? I'll order a 30 inch cheese feast. That will do us all nicely.

HECTOR: Don't order pizza James. I'm hungry now and the pizza wouldn't reach us till dawn.

JAMES sits.

JAMES: I was excited for a cheese feast. Imagine that Bob, a feast of cheese.

BOB: Allergic to cheese me. You two would have a feast, I'd have a funeral.

HECTOR: Tell you what, I'll rustle up some sandwiches, how does that sound?

BOB: Yeah, go on Hector.

HECTOR: What kind would you like?

JAMES: Cheese feast.

HECTOR: No problem, Bob?

BOB: The same please.

HECTOR: Really?

BOB: Really.

There are three loud bangs heard off-stage left. All turn their heads.

JAMES: What was that?

TIMOTHY: *(Off-left)* Hector? Hector are you there?

JAMES: A ghost?

HECTOR: It's Timmy.

JAMES: The apprentice then.

HECTOR: We're in the living room.

JAMES: We're not stupid Hector.

HECTOR: I was talking to Timmy.

JAMES: Then perhaps you need to aim it more directly.

HECTOR: Right you are.

HECTOR turns his head and shouts.

HECTOR: We are in the living room!

TIMOTHY: *(Off-left)* I can't open the door.

JAMES: I'll let him in *(stands)* since I'm standing,

JAMES exits SL.

BOB: Doesn't bode well that he has trouble opening doors does it?

HECTOR: I'm sure there's a valid reason. I do so sometimes let the latch fall when I come in.

BOB: Watch those chickens!

JAMES runs back in, sitting in his seat and looking mighty pale.

HECTOR: Where's the lad?

JAMES vomits into his cup of tea.

HECTOR: That's not really an answer is it Bob?

BOB: No Hector, it's not.

JAMES: Blooming loaf Hector!

HECTOR: What's happening?

TIMOTHY, 18 years old, wearing overalls around his waist, enters. His right arm is covered in shit! He is crying, with a disgusted look on his face.

TIMOTHY: Help me Hector! I can't feel my arm.

BOB: *(To JAMES)* Ten pounds and fifty pence says he hasn't got an arm made out of yummy chocolate!

HECTOR stands and moves cautiously towards the boy.

HECTOR: Timothy lad… what on earth have you been doing in that barn?

TIMOTHY: Get it off me.

HECTOR: I don't understand. You were asked to shovel shit. I pointed to the shovel and described the process.

HECTOR leans forward and sniffs the covered arm.

HECTOR: Oh Mandy Moo, what has this boy done to you? Why Timmy, why?

TIMOTHY: It seemed like something a farmer would do. I should have worn a giant glove but there weren't any to hand, I swear.

BOB: Nightmare image is that, nightmare!

HECTOR: James, go and get me a bucket would you?

JAMES: I need one.

JAMES exits SR, looking remarkably ill.

TIMOTHY: Am I going to die Hector?

HECTOR: No Timothy, but don't touch anyone for 48 hours and don't touch another cow ever again.

TIMOTHY: I'm sorry… only a temperature check I said to myself.

JAMES re-enters with a bucket.

HECTOR: I'm upset with you Timmy, I'm upset with you. Now be off with you and get those shitty fingers out of my sight!

JAMES carefully gives the bucket to TIMOTHY who holds it in his clean hand.

HECTOR: There water in that?

JAMES: And Ultimate Soap!

HECTOR: Good, now into the yard lad and become normal again.

TIMOTHY exits in tears. All three farmers look at each other and shake their heads. Sometimes they retch.

HECTOR: Teething trouble I suppose, never mind. So, cheese feast sandwiches then. You sure about that cheese Bob?

BOB: I am allergic.

JAMES: I can't find my appetite.

HECTOR: I think I'll go have a bath.

BOB: I'd like a wash too.

JAMES: Ultimate Soap does wonders.

HECTOR: Let's all get clean.

Lights down.

THE 2nd SCENE OF THE PLAY CALLED FOUR FARMERS

The four chairs are all empty. HECTOR stands centre stage in his pyjamas, holding the board game, Cluedo!

HECTOR: What could be better on such a bitter, dark night, than a game of the classic detective board game Cluedo?

He starts to take the board and pieces from the box. TIMOTHY enters in a dressing gown, looking shy and worried.

TIMOTHY: I'm all clean now Hector.

HECTOR: What was that?

TIMOTHY: I'm clean.

HECTOR: Good.

TIMOTHY walks to HECTOR and watches as the game is set up on the small table between the chairs.

TIMOTHY: I used to play this when I was smaller.

HECTOR: I'm mad at you Timmy.

TIMOTHY: I thought that you would be.

HECTOR: You're going to be Professor Plum. Because Professor Plum is an arse, and today you've acted like one.

TIMOTHY: Okay Hector.

HECTOR: Sit down.

TIMOTHY: Okay Hector.

TIMOTHY sits on a chair.

TIMOTHY: Who are you going to be?

HECTOR: Miss Scarlett.

TIMOTHY: Why?

HECTOR continues setting up the game, not looking at the lad.

HECTOR: I fancy her don't I!

TIMOTHY: Oh right.

HECTOR: Any problem with that?

TIMOTHY: None.

HECTOR: Good.

Pause.

TIMOTHY: I used to look at one of them characters on the front of a cereal packet. Drew them all of the time, with no clothes on… still holding a bowlful mind.

HECTOR: That's an odd thing to do Timmy.

TIMOTHY: I've always been a bit odd.

TIMOTHY smiles at HECTOR for a long period of time.

HECTOR: I hope it's not the rope. I've played this game ten and a half times and ten of those times it's been that bloody rope.

TIMOTHY: Do you think I have what it takes to be a fully-blown farmer one day?

HECTOR: With more practice and passion, less calling each eye a pervert twin…

TIMOTHY: I don't call my eyes that.

HECTOR: I'm calling them that.

HECTOR pulls out a small mirror from his pyjama pocket and hands it to TIMOTHY.

HECTOR: See for yourself.

TIMOTHY looks into the mirror, prodding an eyeball.

HECTOR: And?

TIMOTHY begins to undo the belt of his dressing gown as he stands.

TIMOTHY: They're telling me to disrobe at once!

Before he can disrobe HECTOR pushes TIMOTHY back down to his sitting position.

HECTOR: Don't listen to them.

TIMOTHY: I see them every day Hector, when I look in the bathroom mirror. That must be why I take so long in there.

HECTOR: You daft cow! I'm only fooling with you. Your eyes are no more perverted than anybody else's.

TIMOTHY: But, what just happened?

HECTOR: Said it yourself Timmy, always been an odd fellow.

TIMOTHY: That's right. And what I tried to do was odd wasn't it?

HECTOR: It was odd. Bob can be Colonel Mustard and James, Mrs White.

JAMES enters wearing pyjamas and his flat cap.

JAMES: Mrs White is the old cook isn't she?

HECTOR: That's the one.

JAMES: I bet she'd do you some bedroom damage that one, with that filthy stare she has. Let me have a look.

JAMES picks up the white playing piece and licks his lips.

JAMES: You know it sweetheart!

HECTOR: The pyjamas fit well.

JAMES puts the piece down and begins to lunge.

JAMES: Like a perfectly fitted glove. If I were to perform such a movement in my own crusty bed wear, I'd have to kiss goodbye to any future children.

HECTOR: You never wanted any did you James?

JAMES: No, and that vasectomy didn't help matters.

HECTOR: What's Bob doing upstairs?

BOB enters wearing a woman's dressing gown.

BOB: Running out of options, that's what.

HECTOR: Is that my wife's dressing gown?

BOB: I bloody well hope so.

HECTOR: Bob, what's wrong with you?

JAMES: What's wrong with you Bob?

TIMOTHY points at BOB.

TIMOTHY: Odd!

HECTOR: Hush Timmy.

BOB: You've only two pairs of pyjamas and a single dressing gown Hector. They were all accounted for. This is what I was left with and boy is it comfortable!

JAMES: Can you lunge in though?

BOB: Let me see.

BOB performs a lunge.

BOB: Could I do such a movement with the woollen monstrosity my wife burdened me with last Christmas? Could I heck, I'd be minus flesh below the waist.

JAMES stands next to BOB.

JAMES: Look at me Bob.

JAMES lunges, BOB lunges, they both lunge.

HECTOR: Now fellas, there's Cluedo to be played.

JAMES: Let's have a lunge-off Bob.

BOB: Later maybe, I've grown a bit tired.

They both sit down.

HECTOR: So, Cluedo then. Watch as I shuffle the cards.

He does so and TIMOTHY applauds him.

HECTOR: Let's hope that rope's a no show.

BOB and JAMES look at each other and shrug. BOB leans over and looks at the board.

BOB: I don't want to be Colonel Mustard.

HECTOR: Yes you do, you love mustard you Bob.

BOB: Not him! I'd like to be Miss Scarlett thank you very much.

HECTOR: You can't be Miss Scarlett.

BOB: Are you playing with her?

HECTOR: I wish!

BOB: Swap with me.

HECTOR: I'd like to but, no, I wouldn't like to do that.

JAMES: Hector, do him a swap.

HECTOR: Why should I?

JAMES: Because I'm about to masturbate, I'm that bored.

TIMOTHY taps HECTOR on the shoulder.

TIMOTHY: Let her go.

HECTOR: Leave it Timmy.

BOB: Swap Hector, come on.

HECTOR: Not on your nelly.

JAMES slowly moves his hand to the top of his pyjama bottoms, about to put a hand down.

JAMES: Oh blimey, look what my hand is trying to do.

HECTOR: Oh alright, have her.

HECTOR kisses the red playing piece.

HECTOR: Good bye sweetheart.

He passes the piece to BOB.

TIMOTHY: Let's simply enjoy the game shall we?

HECTOR: *(To himself)* Don't hit the lad, do not hit him!

JAMES: Go easy on Timothy.

TIMOTHY: It's fine. Hector is in love with Miss Scarlett, that's all.

HECTOR: Telling tales are we Timmy? Mr Snap, Crackle and Cock!

TIMOTHY stands up.

TIMOTHY: How did you know?

HECTOR: A funny guess.

TIMOTHY puts his hands over his eyes.

TIMOTHY: It's these perverted twins in my head. I just like the sounds they make in the milk, what's not to like?

JAMES: Who are the perverted twins? Sounds like a pair I should know about.

TIMOTHY lunges toward JAMES.

TIMOTHY: My eyes James, my *eyes!*

BOB: Nightmare image!

We hear a phone ring from off-stage left.

BOB: Must be the wife Hector.

JAMES: Best answer it.

BOB: Don't tell her what I'm wearing.

HECTOR: I'll get it... it's my phone.

HECTOR exits.

JAMES: Timothy?

TIMOTHY: Yes James?

JAMES: Are you enjoying your apprenticeship?

JAMES puts a hand on TIMOTHY'S leg.

TIMOTHY: I am... I really am. I hope to be a farm one day.

BOB: Thank you.

BOB stands up and claps once before sitting down.

BOB: Thank you very much.

TIMOTHY: Have you both been in the business long?

BOB: Oh a long time, longer than long.

JAMES: Massive.

There is a thud from somewhere outside, followed by the speech of a COW.

JAMES: There's that wind picking up again.

BOB: I was born on a farm I was. Part of a litter of...

JAMES: Bobs?

JAMES slaps his thigh, turning himself on in the process.

JAMES: The world would be a much more miserable place with tens of you plodding around its cabbage patches.

BOB: And my sister is a goat.

TIMOTHY: Really?

BOB: Bleating all night long, ruining birthdays... hard work it was growing up with Hairy Gemma!

TIMOTHY giggles and moves to the window, looking out.

TIMOTHY: Now, that's a sight I have seen.

BOB: What's the lad bleating about?

JAMES: I expect he's trying to change the subject and leave your manure tongue to its own crappy devices.

TIMOTHY: Lots of cows.

BOB: He'll go far this one. I called them daft Dalmatians till I was thirty!

TIMOTHY turns away from the window.

TIMOTHY: Lots of cows outside. And there coming this way.

JAMES: *(To BOB)* Drugs! All the young ones are up to no good. That's what The Farmer Times says.

BOB: Cocaine, heroin... energy drinks!

JAMES: Why would cows be on their way to the farmhouse?

TIMOTHY: I don't know the answer to that James, they are coming though, and with a mean look on their faces.

BOB: Nightmare image!

HECTOR re-enters.

HECTOR: I've got a surprise for you.

JAMES stands.

JAMES: You're not going to seduce us are you?

HECTOR: No, the wife's on her way home.

BOB: Unexpected, but I can't locate the surprise element.

HECTOR: And nobody is being seduced.

BOB: Good! Fiddler!

JAMES: *(Sitting)* What a shame.

TIMOTHY taps HECTOR on the shoulder.

TIMOTHY: Look out of the window Hector.

HECTOR: I'll not fall for that one again sonny Jim. Last time somebody told me to look out a window, I nearly had sex.

JAMES: I've apologised many times for that.

We hear further COW sounds coming from outside.

HECTOR: That sounds like Bessie.

HECTOR goes to the window.

HECTOR: It is Bessie! How the crackers did she get out?

TIMOTHY: Cows have legs Hector, four of them.

BOB: Greedy bastards!

TIMOTHY: *(To BOB)* But they don't have any arms.

BOB: Poor bastards!

HECTOR: Let's try and forget about the cows and play a lovely game before Mrs Constant Nag re-enters my life.

TIMOTHY: But what about the cows?

HECTOR: Sit down.

They all take a seat, HECTOR is on his knees.

HECTOR: Now Cluedo is one of those games that involves patience, an eye for a red herring, dastardly weapons and a dash of travelling round squares.

BOB: I'm so excited about this.

JAMES: Me too.

JAMES drinks from his hip flask. The COWS outside go 'Moo!' TIMOTHY stands but HECTOR pulls him back down to a sitting position.

HECTOR: Don't worry about the cows and concentrate on the game. Bessie will keep the others right. Now, Professor Plum goes first, so roll the dice.

TIMOTHY rolls the dice as JAMES downs his flask, looking a tad worse for wear.

TIMOTHY: Two sixes Hector.

HECTOR: Nobody likes a smart arse Timmy, nobody.

TIMOTHY: *(To BOB)* It's Timothy, that's my name.

BOB: *(Says them both the same)* Potato – potato!

Six loud bangs come from outside.

JAMES: That's one angry wind, knocking like that.

TIMOTHY: I don't think it's the wind that's a knocking.

There is one single 'Moo!'

TIMOTHY: In fact, I'm certain that's not the wind that's a knocking.

HECTOR: Bessie? Bessie is that you?

HECTOR walks to SL, calling off-stage.

HECTOR: You best answer me Bessie.

There is a pause and then a single 'Moo!'

HECTOR: That's better.

TIMOTHY: How does he know?

JAMES: Got a good rapport with his cows Hector has. It's because he keeps them so well.

BOB: He does keep them well.

JAMES: Oh, he does.

HECTOR: Now Bessie, what are you doing out of the barn at this time of night?

BESSIE 'Moos!' her story.

HECTOR: No, that's not good at all.

More comes from BESSIE and HECTOR turns to TIMOTHY.

HECTOR: Oh dear.

TIMOTHY: What's wrong?

HECTOR: Dear, dear, oh dear, silly Timmy.

JAMES: *(To BOB)* Sounds serious.

TIMOTHY: Have I done something wrong?

HECTOR: The cow you put an arm up?

TIMOTHY: It was on a BBC2 documentary I swear.

HECTOR: That was Bessie's sister, Carol.

BOB: Not Carol! *(To TIMOTHY)* You filthy swine!

TIMOTHY: Tell Carol I'm sorry.

JAMES: It's no good lad.

TIMOTHY moves toward HECTOR but JAMES holds him back.

TIMOTHY: *(Shouting off)* I'm sorry Carol.

HECTOR: Bessie's mad at you Timmy, really mad. She's a right mad cow at this point.

There is the sound of a car alarm from outside. JAMES rushes to the window SR, a little drunk.

JAMES: A gang of cows have ruined your car Hector.

HECTOR: It was old anyway.

We now hear the sound of a 'Moo!' followed by a huge explosion.

JAMES: They've blown up your barn Hector.

BOB: Ruffian beasts! Where will they live?

TIMOTHY: I'm so sorry Hector.

BESSIE speaks from outside.

HECTOR: No Bessie, no! That's enough madness for one evening. Let us call the fire brigade and play Cluedo in peace.

'Moo!'

HECTOR: She wants you to go outside Timmy.

JAMES: Sounds about right. They're clapping their hooves together like an intent animal army.

BOB: You can't send the lad out to face that mob. They'll eat him alive… or at least shit on his face!

'Moo!'

HECTOR: Bessie said she'd never stoop so low. But she and her cow army have planted milky explosives around the house.

'Moo!'

HECTOR: She's giving us eight minutes till she presses the udder!

BOB: Nightmare image!

JAMES: This is madness Hector.

HECTOR: No James, this is being a farmer.

TIMOTHY holds his head up high and goes to HECTOR.

TIMOTHY: I'll go. It's my fault; it was me who fiddled with Carol.

JAMES: You don't have to. Let that butter churn, I hate the fuck out of Cluedo anyway.

BOB: They're only cows… hundreds of mad, bloodthirsty cows!

TIMOTHY: Hector?

HECTOR: You do what you think right and true. But I really like my house and my wife has finished her knitting and is on her way home so…

TIMOTHY: I understand.

TIMOTHY turns to JAMES and BOB.

TIMOTHY: It was a pleasure meeting you both.

BOB: And you lad, you would have made one hell of a good farm.

JAMES: *(In tears)* I'll miss you a tractor full.

TIMOTHY heads to the door before turning back.

TIMOTHY: Goodbye everyone.

He leaves. The others bow their heads as we hear a great big 'Moo!'

JAMES: Will he be okay?

We hear the sound of TIMOTHY getting beaten up by a bunch cows.

HECTOR: I'm sure he will be.

BOB: Positive thoughts everybody.

TIMOTHY: *(Off-stage)* Hector! Bessie is taking me to the swamp, said she's going to learn me how to swim.

BOB: Positive thoughts.

They all sit down.

HECTOR: Let's all forget about whatever it is I've just forgotten about and solve us a murder or two.

BOB: Put the kettle on Hector.

HECTOR: Oooarrrhh! Right you are Bob.

HECTOR exits with a strange look on his face.

A pause or two happens.

JAMES: He keeps us well does Hector.

BOB: He does keep us well.

JAMES / BOB: Very well.

The lights fade as BOB picks up the rope from the game board. JAMES grows bored and before he can put a hand down his pyjama bottoms we...

BLACKOUT

The End

That Creeper Man Dance

Written by Alan Pickthall 2014

Characters

Arthur

Mrs Froggington

Carol

Samuel Trick

Sir Naff

Lady Shiver

SCENE ONE

Lights slowly fade up as a man staggers across the back of the stage. He seems quite the drunkard, though when he gets to the centre, he stops, notices the audience, comes forward to centre and waves to a few people.

ARTHUR: Good evening; I'm an actor!

ARTHUR coughs, warming himself up for his dialogue.

ARTHUR: To make the statement that Twiddlington was a typical English village would be but a mistake. Of course it looked as much a village as most villages do, with a main cobbled road where a post office, shop, church and pub all stood. Well, indeed they still stand, smug as you like.

He drinks from a bottle.

ARTHUR: Many a terraced house there is, with the odd thatched roof abode still standing. Only one or two grand houses, where the 'well to do' and 'done well' park their posh bottoms. There is an allotment where, perhaps the more filthy-arsed congregate within their vegetable kingdom.

He staggers forward to the front – burps three times.

ARTHUR: Cucumbers! I can only presume most villages are invigorated by the odd scandal and that Twiddlington is no different. Unhappy spinsters clacking the tongues about darling idiots from behind many net curtains! Same everywhere, the actual same I'm sure. There is one thing I do hope sets this place apart… Shady Lane! A lane upon which an alleyway leads downward to a foul back wall… away… slightly, from the daily passers-by… where a man dances slowly, a facial expression fixed, looking toward you… eyes never leaving… leaves blow around his feet, no strength in them to knock him from his dancing… he carries on.

Behind ARTHUR, two chairs appear, not by magic, no, but by the characters who will sit on them. MRS FROGGINGTON and her friend CAROL enter SR – Mrs Froggington is made-up to look almost pantomime-like, whilst Carol is plain as can be, though she does sip tea from a teapot. They stand behind chairs.

ARTHUR: Behind me, an off-beat home, a lilac abode, where one Mrs Froggington sits with her friend, Carol. Mrs Froggington of Twiddlington; she likes the similar sound of both name and town, however much she catches herself wishing she could be plonked on…

MRS FROGGINGTON: Chedderton Lane!

ARTHUR: And not…

CAROL: Wispy Way!

ARTHUR: But you can't and won't have everything can you?

ARTHUR exits, swigging from his bottle. The two women sit.

MRS FROGGINGTON: I do love a Tuesday.

CAROL: You do?

MRS FROGGINGTON: Masses of 'yes' to the loving of Tuesdays Carol.

CAROL: For what reason?

MRS FROGGINGTON: Don't be perturbed Carol. I've nothing against Mondays, and Wednesdays my mate, but it's only the truth that Tuesdays strike me as best.

CAROL: It gladdens me that you hold the enthusiasm that you do, for a day of the week.

MRS FROGGINGTON: Of course I can't stay wanting for a husband who has forward-dived into the graveyard. I would love to but my emotions move far too quickly for that.

MRS FROGGINGTON leans rapidly toward CAROL, pointing at her in a threatening manner.

MRS FROGGINGTON: Do you understand me Carol?

CAROL: *(A tad scared)* I do certainly.

MRS FROGGINGTON calms and ruffles the hair of CAROL.

MRS FROGGINGTON: Good that's why we are friends.

CAROL: Soul mates!

MRS FROGGINGTON: I like you Carol but no!

CAROL: Oh!

They both drink – a knock from SR.

SAMUEL: *(Off-stage)* Telegram for Mrs Froggington.

MRS FROGGINGTON stands, shuffling her bosom and practising a pouted lip.

CAROL: What are you doing Mrs Froggington?

MRS FROGGINGTON: You are one nosey bitch aren't you Carol? But if you must know, I was shuffling my bosom and partaking in the perfect art of practicing a pouted lip.

SAMUEL: *(Off-stage)* Mrs Froggington? A telegram for you!

CAROL and MRS FROGGINGTON exchange glances.

MRS FROGGINGTON: Do come in Samuel.

CAROL: Samuel?

MRS FROGGINGTON: Telegram Samuel!

ARTHUR re-enters with SAMUEL, the telegram boy behind him.

ARTHUR: Samuel Trick, eighteen, delivering the weekly telegram sent from Mrs Froggington's sister over in Punktown!

ARTHUR stands to the side and watches the scene.

SAMUEL: I have your telegram Mrs Froggington.

MRS FROGGINGTON: I know that, for it is a Tuesday. And my sister just loves to give the Punktown gossip! I wonder what the Vicar said? What did Mrs Hitchcock reveal? Who murdered Mr Brambles a second time?

CAROL: Saucy.

MRS FROGGINGTON: Samuel?

SAMUEL: Yes Mrs F?

MRS FROGGINGTON: Hello there.

SAMUEL: Hello.

MRS FROGGINGTON: I love you.

SAMUEL: Excuse me?

MRS FROGGINGTON: I'd love you to have some cake – I made it before I entered this very scene.

SAMUEL: No thanks, best be off. Goodbye Mrs Froggington.

SAMUEL exits and ARTHUR follows him.

MRS FROGGINGTON: Goodbye, my main man!

MRS FROGGINGTON sits with the telegram in her hands. CAROL is about to open her mouth.

MRS FROGGINGTON: Don't say a thing please Carol.

CAROL: I'll not say a word. I'll not rock the tail feathers or ruffle any boats! Or beat on the brat, beat on the brat with a baseball bat, by Ramones, oh yeah!

MRS FROGGINGTON: That's saying things Carol.

MRS FROGGINGTON exits in a huff. CAROL is all alone.

CAROL: Yes… yes, I suppose it was. Silly Carol.

CAROL sips from the teapot.

LIGHTS FADE as she giggles.

SCENE TWO

The chairs have been taken so that the stage is bare. SAMUEL TRICK enters SL, humming a tune and kicking at loose stones. ARTHUR enters up-stage, following the lad.

ARTHUR: Let us all observe young Samuel Trick, dawdling down Wispy Way, heading out on to Shady Lane where tall trees tower over cobbles, giving the place only a part of its name. The boy passes an alleyway that runs between two houses, both have the curtains drawn. Samuel feels something.

SAMUEL shivers, stops and regains himself.

ARTHUR: He puts it down to…

SAMUEL: A shiver…

ARTHUR: Nothing but…

SAMUEL: A breeze!

ARTHUR: Unaware that he is being watched.

SAMUEL removes a pair of binoculars from his pocket.

ARTHUR: I know of him. These binoculars have been used many times before this particular Tuesday.

SAMUEL pushes past an old man, SIR NAFF, who has entered SR, carrying a stuffed dog.

SIR NAFF: Watch where you're going.

SAMUEL and ARTHUR exit.

SIR NAFF: Bloody boy racers! Walking, no, running everywhere as if their lazy bones had some place to be. What's becoming of

Twiddlington Fifi? This village used to be paced so leisurely, ah well, needn't worry… you'll be home soon enough.

SIR NAFF puts 'Fifi' down on to the ground.

SIR NAFF: Look at that! Curtains closed and not much after lunch time. How bizarre folk are sometimes… if it's not a youth moving at a devil speed, it is persons unknown closing curtains during the most lit part of the day. What next? The bowling green painted a merry shade of red?

He looks down at 'Fifi.'

SIR NAFF: I love you.

He looks toward the audience.

SIR NAFF: Who on earth is that? And why is he moving so? I say, can I be of any assistance dear fellow? My name is…

He stops, caught in a daze. As he stares, SIR NAFF slowly starts to sway his arms – lights fade on him.

SCENE THREE

A lady in nice clothes is central and in a bit of a panic. She is LADY SHIVER.

LADY SHIVER: He's gone mad – mad he's gone! My once non-baffled husband is now raving in his bedroom, raving mad and performing a dance I can only call a rave!

MRS FROGGINGTON enters, rushing in. CAROL follows, timidly, behind her.

MRS FROGGINGTON: I'm here darling, how is he?

LADY SHIVER: About as good as something awful I'm afraid.

MRS FROGGINGTON: How awful!

LADY SHIVER: I have tried to snap him out of it, but he only continues to move as a lunatic. *(Noticing Carol)* Hello Carol.

CAROL: *(Nods)* Lady Shiver.

LADY SHIVER shivers and rubs her arms.

LADY SHIVER: Mrs Froggington I cannot tell you how useless I feel.

MRS FROGGINGTON: Have you telephoned Doctor Blank?

LADY SHIVER: Yes.

MRS FROGGINGTON: And what did he suggest?

LADY SHIVER: He laughed and put the phone down.

MRS FROGGINGTON: *(To Carol)* He really should be struck off you know?

CAROL: Right off!

MRS FROGGINGTON: Let us not get too worried. A biscuit will see you fine, a biscuit followed by a waterfall of thirst-quenching tea leaves with added water.

LADY SHIVER: You talk of additional water and yet Sir Naff has danced for over three hours without one bead of sweat upon his brow.

MRS FROGGINGTON: Can we see him? Perhaps me and Carol can help?

LADY SHIVER: Please do, I'm at a loss. I have a clue that I have not one in terms of a cure.

MRS FROGGINGTON: Carol my dear?

CAROL: After you.

MRS FROGGINGTON: Let us go and observe Sir Naff and his 'sounds odd' condition.

Lights fade as they all walk off!

SCENE FOUR

A bedroom – SIR NAFF, once pompous and rigid, is now fluid and jelly-boned, dancing it up big-style.

LADY SHIVER: Darling Naffy? I have Mrs Froggington and Carol with me.

He continues to dance.

MRS FROGGINGTON: He's dancing.

CAROL: To no music, none at all.

LADY SHIVER: See how fluid and jelly-boned he is? Goodbye arthritis, I thought at first. But without pause for breath I worry Sir Naff may waltz himself into the grave.

MRS FROGGINGTON: The situation does seem almost bleak. Carol?

CAROL: Yes Mrs Froggington?

MRS FROGGINGTON: What do you think?

CAROL: He's dancing quite a lot?

MRS FROGGINGTON nods in agreement – LADY SHIVER bursts into tears.

MRS FROGGINGTON: What's wrong with Lady Shiver?

LADY SHIVER points to the dancing man.

MRS FROGGINGTON: Of course, yes.

CAROL: Allow me to perform an idea I have had.

LADY SHIVER cries on MRS FROGGINGTON'S shoulder.

MRS FROGGINGTON: Go on Carol, perform your idea.

CAROL stretches and moves to SIR NAFF in a most confident fashion.

CAROL: Sir Naff?

He dances unaware of her.

CAROL: Cease this silliness Sir Naff. Look at what you've done to your once beautiful wife. Lady Shiver's a mess!

This makes LADY SHIVER cry harder.

CAROL: No response? Then you leave me with very little bits of choice!

CAROL grabs SIR NAFF'S shoulders and attempts holding him still. This doesn't work and she ends up on his shoulders as he raves like the very best of ravers.

MRS FROGGINGTON and then LADY SHIVER fuss around them, circling but afraid to touch.

CAROL: My idea seems to have lacked success.

MRS FROGGINGTON: I am afraid that I must agree with you Carol.

CAROL: What should I do?

MRS FROGGINGTON: Ride it out Carol.

CAROL: But he won't stop!

LADY SHIVER: Throw a whisper into his earlobes; he hates that more than anything, except loosing on the races.

CAROL does as instructed. This does not work.

CAROL: Ideas are dwindling.

Somehow CAROL is moved around SIR NAFF'S person till she is stood once more on the floor. They both begin to Foxtrot.

MRS FROGGINGTON: My word!

LADY SHIVER: *(Pointing)* What is this?

MRS FROGGINGTON: The Foxtrot at a glance… perhaps a smidgeon of Tango!

LADY SHIVER: Confound that Tango! Damn be to the Foxtrot!

MRS FROGGINGTON: I wouldn't go so far as to damn the Foxtrot Lady Shiver, but yes, the Tango is an arsehole of a dance and has no place in Twiddlington!

CAROL: Hear, hear!

LADY SHIVER: What should we do?

MRS FROGGINGTON: Just watch I suppose.

ARTHUR enters as all of this goes on behind him. He stands SL looking mighty pleased with himself.

ARTHUR: And so Lady Shiver and Mrs Froggington watched the unhappy couple, Sir Naff and Carol, dance a bad one, not realising that worry had transformed into admiration.

LADY SHIVER and MRS FROGGINGTON both applaud the dance – MRS F holds up an 8 whilst LADY S gives them a great big 9!

ARTHUR: Would they be surprised to learn that in another eight rooms of drawing, living and bed… eight more sorry dancing souls were gyrating to an undisclosed beat? Maybe they would be? But I'm not surprised, not a flower am I surprised one bit. Because I know that Sir Naff is the ninth 'mover' – the ninth of many more indeed. I am not an actor and my name is not Arthur; I am not really here…

ARTHUR screams and the other characters ignore him.

ARTHUR: See? I'm for your eyes and ears only. I am stood, as a matter of fact, and a fact of matter, with my feet firmly placed at the bottom of an alleyway. Not far from here and dancing… dancing, constantly… like this…

ARTHUR begins to dance, swaying his arms from left to right – a merry jig if ever there was one.

LIGHTS FADE ON HIM.

SCENE FIVE

SAMUEL TRICK is stood CS, peering into the audience.

SAMUEL: Are you okay down there?

No response.

SAMUEL: Do you need any help? Because I can go get PC Clover, he's the best on the beat!

No response.

SAMUEL: He's the best on the beat… PC Clover, he's the best on the beat… beat… beat, best on the beat…

SAMUEL lifts his arms and begins to sway them.

SAMUEL: Beat, beat, creeper man, beat… best on the…

LIGHTS DOWN

MUSIC

LIGHTS UP

SAMUEL is joined by SIR NAFF, MRS FROGGINGTON, CAROL and LADY SHIVER; they all dance.

The CREEPER MAN / ARTHUR faces them, dancing, from within the audience itself and laughs like a right bad egg.

LIGHTS SLOWLY FADE AS THE MUSIC DROWNS OUT THE LAUGHTER.

END.

Insomniac Clowns

Written by Alan Pickthall 2011

Characters

Marcus *(a clown)*

Benny *(a clown)*

Mr Hickling *(the manager of 'Naked Bargains')*

Martha *(an older employee)*

Jimmy *(a young employee)*

(The Host)

The sound of a snowy blizzard.

This goes into annoying supermarket music – LIGHTS UP

MR HICKLING enters with a marker pen in one hand and 'offer' signs in the other.

MR HICKLING: This is a joke!

He writes a price on one of the signs.

MR HICKLING: Cutting prices once again, I'm a self-harmer alright. Soon I'll be a Pound Shop, a 50p shop, heavens! Hey ho, however, needs be in order to survive this most terrible economic weather. *(Sighs, writes on another sign)* Soon, I'll be put in one of those lunatic cottages for the middle-aged, talking to myself like I'm in some silly play!

MR HICKLING goes to SL and picks up a dummy head from one of the boxes. He puts signs and pens in his pockets, clutching the head in both hands.

MR HICKLING: Luckily I have you Carol. Carol and you have me. I promise if this supermarket becomes a recession casualty, we're off to sunny Mexico!

Holds head up so he is face to face with it.

MR HICKLING: Or Plymouth. I have family there.

He kisses 'CAROL' on the cheek. JIMMY, a teenage lad enters. MR HICKLING holds the head up into the air.

MR HICKLING: 'To be or not to…'

JIMMY: Yeah whatever.

JIMMY goes up-stage and starts to get ready for his shift.

MR HICKLING: *(At watch)* Twilight shift begins in 5 minutes. I'm sorry Carol, you'll simply have to wait.

He holds the head down at crotch level.

MR HICKLING: Fuck I'm in love!

MARTHA, an older lady, enters with a shopping bag.

MARTHA: Evening.

MR HICKLING keeps the head where it is as he greets MARTHA; he thrusts subtlety now and again.

MR HICKLING: Good evening Martha how are you?

MARTHA: Ready as I'll ever be.

MR HICKLING: As you'll ever be? So you'll never actually get any better?

MARTHA: You've seen the best of me boss, it's 'fair to middling' all the way from now on.

She joins JIMMY at the back of the stage, getting ready. MR HICKLING holds 'CAROL' up and wipes her lips.

MR HICKLING: Look what I have to work with.

He places the dummy head back into the box.

MR HICKLING: *(At watch)* Team Twilight!

JIMMY and MARTHA stand next to MR HICKLING.

MARTHA: Here I be, ready to count, stack and face.

JIMMY: Yeah, whatever!

MR HICKLING: Thank you both for coming. I recognise that the snow has made it fairly hazardous for some, indeed Brian died trying to get here.

MARTHA: What?

JIMMY: Ever?

MR HICKLING: I know it's sad, but let us look to the future. We have eight pallets to get on the shop floor between now and seven a.m. So let's keep smiling eh?

Creepy circus music plays as all characters freeze.

BENNY AND MARCUS enter. Benny stood DSR, MARCUS DSL. They are both wearing clown make-up and are in the middle of getting ready. BENNY is brushing his teeth. Both are on phones.

BENNY: Wi we shouwds nalls!

MARCUS: What was that?

BENNY: *(Toothbrush out)* I need some balls.

MARCUS: Juggling balls?

BENNY: That's right.

MARCUS: We don't any.

BENNY: Marcus, we're clowns. You've not thought this through.

MARCUS: Of course I have. *(Tries to keep voice down)* I have this planned to a 'T.'

BENNY: A 'T?'

MARCUS: We've got thirty minutes, then you've got to meet me down the alley.

BENNY: I'm not meeting you in an alley, you pervert.

MARCUS: *(Trying to stay calm)* Look, I'm not bumming you! The alley is next to the car park, which is next to the supermarket.

BENNY: Interesting.

MARCUS: *(Losing patience)* There's nothing interesting about it, its common sense. Meet me in half an hour.

BENNY: It's still snowing outside. We should have bought some of those clodhoppers, ski's or shoes.

BENNY looks up at the ceiling.

MARCUS: We'll be fine, I've got a copy of the bakery door key so they'll not even notice. The alarm won't be on, so nothing's a problem, okay? Benny? Don't be falling asleep on me, Benny!

BENNY: *(Snapping out of it)* Yes, or Benjamin, whatever you fancy. I don't mind or care.

MARCUS: You're okay with all of this, you agree?

BENNY: Lots of per cent Marcus, it was wrong what they did to you. There was a face in my ceiling but I'm back in the room.

MARCUS: The ceiling? Benny don't be late.

BENNY: Not a chance.

MARCUS: You're a bloody great mate you, don't I always tell you?

BENNY: Nope.

MARCUS: Thirty minutes okay? *(At watch)* Twenty-five now, half ten, alleyway, see you there.

MARCUS hangs up and goes to the back corner of the stage, getting ready. BENNY looks at the ceiling again.

BENNY: It has a crooked smile!

SUPERMARKET MUSIC – BENNY goes to the opposite back corner of the stage and gets ready.

JIMMY and MARTHA stand centre-stage and use case knives to mime opening trays and stacking tins as they talk.

MARTHA: So, how's college?

JIMMY: Crap!

MARTHA: Your family?

JIMMY: Crap!

MARTHA: Are you courting?

JIMMY: *(Looks at her)* Don't speak French!

MARTHA: *(Shivers)* Is there a door open somewhere?

They continue to work, one gazes at the other. MR HICKLING walks between them, looks at their stacking.

MR HICKLING: Well done Martha, some most excellent stacking right there. Though what have I said, do you remember?

MARTHA: *(Head down)* Beware the barcode!

MR HICKLING: *Beware the barcode! Love* the label, that's what attracts.

MARTHA: Oh, Mr Hickling, I know.

MR HICKLING looks at JIMMY's work.

MR HICKLING: Now Jimmy, there's a word in my mouth and I want rid, you have some idea what it is?

JIMMY: Crap!

MR HICKLING: Yes! Worrying work I have to say, dent's everywhere you look.

JIMMY: Well, you've got to open the tin to eat it!

MR HICKLING slaps JIMMY on the back of the head.

MR HICKLING: I'm deducting an hour's wage, from your wage!

MARTHA: You can't do that, there's one of those economical thingamabob's happening.

MR HICKLING: Don't I know it! Two staff on a twilight shift? I must be terribly mental, I really must.

BENNY and MARCUS enter SL and MARTHA, MR HICKLING and JIMMY stand close to each other stage-right, Martha screams.

MARTHA: I hate clowns.

JIMMY: This is crap!

MR HICKLING: What's the ruddy meaning of this?

Marcus is the more assertive of the two clowns (for both boys – 18, are dressed as such. Marcus has red hair, Benny has blue) Marcus holds a gun in his hand and holds it up into the air.

MARCUS: Everybody just chill the heck out, this is a bit of a robbery.

BENNY holds his hands in the shape of a gun. He is the most unhinged of the pair. He points his pistol-hands at the three twilight-workers who all hold their hands up.

BENNY: If any of you fucking pricks move… I'll slap every one of you on the bottom.

JIMMY is the same age as the two clowns.

JIMMY: Calm down will you? I really can't be bothered with any trouble today.

BENNY: He can't be bothered with trouble. Did you hear that?

MARCUS: I did yes. No trouble you say?

JIMMY: That's it, whatever!

MARCUS lowers his gun and becomes almost apologetic.

MARCUS: Are you sure?

JIMMY: *(Unsure)* Erm… yes.

MARCUS: You should have said so before, so sorry to bother you.

BENNY: Off we pop!

Both clowns wave and exit the stage, whistling!
JIMMY, MR HICKLING and MARTHA wait a moment and then lower their hands. They breathe a collective sigh of relief.
They are about to smile when BENNY and MARCUS run back on, each brandishing their own version of 'gun.' Marcus moves toward Mr Hickling and holds the pistol to his temple. Benny slaps Jimmy on the arse.

BENNY: What did I tell you?

MARCUS: That was a trick! As if we'd give up that easily.

BENNY: *(Points to costumes)* Especially when we've gone to so much trouble and effort.

MARCUS: That's right, Bonnie and Clyde never gave it this much thought.

BENNY: Though I'd have given Faye Dunnaway a right old kiss and cuddle, if you know what I mean?

MARCUS: Bloody me an all, 'phwoar-some' she was, God bless her.

BENNY: Not at the same time though, we're mates and everything, but not *that* kind of mates.

MARCUS: True. Now, who's going to be a helpful girl or boy and open the safe?

MR HICKLING: Please don't hurt us.

MARCUS: Mr Hickling, the manager of this supermarket are you not?

MR HICKLING: I am indeed.

MARCUS: So you can provide a question with an appropriate answer? You are capable?

MARTHA: Leave him alone, didn't your mother teach you not to be so rude?

BENNY turns his gaze on MARTHA.

BENNY: So the old witch does have a voice; I thought you'd lost it along with your teeth!

MR HICKLING: How dare you speak to Martha like that?

BENNY: So the little bit of manager has the hots for his twilight lady of the night!

JIMMY: Don't speak to Mr Hickling like that.

BENNY: Oh, so the young master Jimmy of the newly-checkout-trained-status young 'un has a man-crush on the boss? Got news for you Jimmy – overtimes full!

MARTHA: Don't speak to young Jimmy like that.

BENNY: So the old witch does have a voice, she been knitting pants for you Jimmy?

JIMMY: No, mine are cotton innit!

MR HICKLING: How dare you speak to Jimmy like that?

MARCUS: *(Shouts)* Everybody just… *shut* up, now! *(Pause)* Thank you very much.

BENNY: So the little bit of manager helps with knitting does he?

MARCUS: *(Snaps)* Zip lips!

BENNY: Okay buddy, together they go.

BENNY bites his bottom lip

MARCUS: There we go.

MR HICKLING: What is the point of all this? Is it money you're after?

MARCUS: *(Straight-faced)* No, I've come for three tins of beans, two packs of ham and some fishy fucking fingers! Money, that's what I want. And not any money, no no no, *my* money.

MR HICKLING: Your money?

MARCUS: So this really isn't a robbery at all. One of sorts I suppose but not typically so. I'd much prefer to call this collecting on an IOU!

MR HICKLING: I... O... U...?

MARCUS: You do yes, I'm glad we're reading from the same page.

BENNY: Drinking from the same cup of tea.

MARCUS: Quite.

BENNY: Singing the same dastardly hymn.

MARCUS: Thanks Benny.

BENNY: Jacking off over the same jazz-mag!

MARCUS: *(Turning head)* Benny, thank-*you!*

BENNY: My lips are little shits...

JIMMY: I don't see how this supermarket owes you anything.

MARCUS: But it does... lots!

MARCUS moves up close to MARTHA who shuts her eyes.

MARTHA: I hate clowns.

MARCUS: Good.

MARTHA: Even more now one has a gun pointed at my face.

MARCUS has indeed done this very thing.

MARCUS: I call it a 'face-point', don't I?

BENNY doesn't respond.

MARCUS: I do anyway; tends to make even the sweat *sweat*!

MARTHA: I'll take your word for it.

MARCUS: Don't take my word for it.

He rubs a finger over her forehead and inspects his fingertip.

MARCUS: Clammy!

MR HICKLING: You cowardly boy…

MARCUS: *Nervous* aren't you Martha? Don't worry, so am I. I've never used a gun before in my life and it's so awfully close to your jaw… not a *huge* gossip are you? And Mr Hickling, be careful on the coward-front…

MARCUS moves the gun from MARTHA to MR HICKLING.

MARCUS: I'm not best friends with that word, not at all. Am I?

He's again talking to BENNY who stands facing the audience, not paying attention. Instead of answering, he eats from a bag of popcorn he has picked up from the side of the stage.

MARCUS: *Am I?*

The CAST freeze apart from BENNY who hums a tune as he munches his popcorn.

Apart from MARCUS, the other three act as voices for THE HOST, coming out of the freeze-frame momentarily when delivering lines.

THE HOST: *(Mr Hickling)* Benny?

BENNY hears this but shrugs it off.

THE HOST: *(Martha)* Benny!

BENNY: Quiet, I'm eating popcorn.

THE HOST

THE HOST: *(Jimmy & Martha)* Benjamin!

BENNY: *(Turns head)* What?

THE HOST: *(Jimmy)* Hi Benny.

BENNY: Who are you?

THE HOST: *(Jimmy)* Have you missed me?

BENNY: I don't know you, how could I have *missed* you?

THE HOST: *(Mr Hickling)* I've been around awhile now.

BENNY: Have you?

THE HOST: *(Mr Hickling)* Yes, are you ready for your interview?

THE HOST takes a microphone out of his pocket and holds it up, smiling at BENNY looks at it, unsure.

BENNY: Not really mate.

THE HOST looks down at the microphone and then back up at BENNY, fake smiling.

THE HOST: *(Martha - Softly)* No problem, whenever you're ready.

THE HOST leaves the other characters.

BENNY: Yeah, do one will you!

The rest of the cast unfreeze.

MARCUS: I won't be doing one thank you very much. I'm asking you a question.

BENNY still looks at the corner of the stage.

MARCUS: Benny?

BENNY: *(Looks at Marcus)* Yes Marcus?

MARCUS: Am I?

BENNY: That's your name I believe.

MARCUS: No, *am* I? Friends with that word?

BENNY: Which one?

MARCUS: Coward.

BENNY: Oh grow up Marcus; there are bigger things to worry about.

BENNY points to the staff.

MARCUS: You're right… wait!

BENNY: What?

MARCUS rushes up to BENNY and slaps him across the face. BENNY rubs his shocked face.

BENNY: What in Jenny Éclair's name!

MARCUS: *(Keeping quiet)* You used my name you nana; we decided on the Two Ronnie's, Corbett for you, Barker for me. You used my *name.*

BENNY: You used my name.

MARCUS: That's utterly false Benny.

BENNY: You did, lots of times, and just this moment too. *(To the staff)* Didn't he?

JIMMY: You did, his name's Benny.

MARTHA: Jimmy stay out of it.

MR HICLKING: Let's all be quiet shall we? We don't want to rile them anymore.

MARCUS: Well this is great. We've given our real names away, we're dressed in these ridiculous outfits.

BENNY: They were your idea.

MARCUS: *(Thinks)* That may be, but they were a notch-up from your idea I suppose.

BENNY: Were not.

MARCUS: So you think that disguising ourselves as two naturists would have protected our identity more than these?

BENNY: They weren't meant to be disguises as such. But our sheer nakedness would have made them forget who the people were.

MARCUS: Does that actually *mean* anything?

BENNY: If there's a naked person in front of you, you don't look above the neck do you?

MARCUS: That wouldn't work you simple bastard.

BENNY: It's worked for me plenty of times.

MARCUS: Really?

BENNY: I have it on tape.

Pause

MARCUS: This is getting us nowhere.

MARCUS turns to the staff and points the gun at all of them.

MARCUS: All of you, on the floor.

MARTHA: It's dirty.

MARCUS: Lick it clean then, on the floor, now!

MR HICKLING: How dare you speak to a lady of an advanced number of years like that. You should respect your elders boyo…

BENNY: So the little bit of manager has the hots for his twilight lady of the night!

MARCUS looks at BENNY and puts a hand on his shoulder.

MARCUS: I think we've been there already.

BENNY: Not enough in my book, let's hurt one of them.

MARCUS: And which one do you think we should hurt?

MARCUS looks at the staff who are still standing.

MARCUS: I'm sorry, I must have forgotten to introduce you to the floor.

JIMMY: You're not that good at this robbery malarkey are you?

MARCUS: *(Shouts)* FLOOR.

The staff move to the floor, MARTHA moves slower than the others.
BENNY and MARCUS circle them once they are all laid down.

BENNY: All of them.

MARCUS: We're not hurting all of them. The hurting is supposed to act as a warning so that the others know we mean business. Then they cooperate.

BENNY: You've read a book haven't you?

MARCUS: BBC 2 documentary.

BENNY: Fine, I'm going to dip to decide the fists target.

BENNY stands behind them and uses his fingers to point, like a gun again.

BENNY: *(As a rhyme)*
'Eanie-meanie
Baked Beanie
Open the tin
And put it in
Your mouth
Ouch, it's hot
Should have waited
You great big slut
Blow them cool
Yum yum
Chow on down
Rub your tum
Nice nice
Nice nice

<blockquote>
Oh yes
Beans are my favourite.'
</blockquote>

He ends pointing at MR HICKLING.

BENNY: Let's hurt the little bit.

He changes to JIMMY.

JIMMY: That didn't land on me.

BENNY: It's my finger; it can point to whomever it likes. Blame the finger!

MARCUS: That's very true.

JIMMY: Totally not fair.

MARCUS: Nice little rhyme you had there.

BENNY: I thought of it all by myself one cold and lonely night.

MARCUS: I'd have maybe changed the last line.

BENNY: Would you?

MARCUS: Yes.

BENNY: To what?

MARCUS: Beans are the best goes better with 'oh yes' than 'beans are my favourite'. 'Oh yes, beans are the best!' See?

BENNY: But they are my favourite.

MARCUS: I know that, you know that and me and you both smell that. Best is more pleasing to the ear that's all.

BENNY considers this for a moment, a tad upset.

JIMMY: Are you going to hurt me or what?

MARCUS: In a minute, just relax okay?

JIMMY lies on his back and puts his arms behind his head as if he were sunbathing.

BENNY: How about?

MARCUS: Quickly…

BENNY: (*As a rhyme*)
>'Nice nice
>Nice nice
>Oh yes
>Go fuck yourself!'

MARCUS: I'd say it needs some work.

BENNY gets to his knees and starts to strangle JIMMY. MARTHA and MR HICKLING protest a bit but soon give up.

MARCUS: Get off him Benny.

BENNY continues the strangulation.

MR HICKLING: *(to Martha)* I really should have locked the front door before the shift began.

MARTHA: Oh the horror, the *horror!*

MARCUS reaches down and pulls BENNY off of JIMMY, Benny's hands are still held in the shape of Jimmy's neck.

MARCUS: Calm down would you?

BENNY: I'm fine now Marcus. I just needed to get rid of some tension.

MARCUS stands BENNY up.

MARCUS: Behave yourself and *stop* using my *name*.

BENNY: It's too late for that I think. Why don't you go to the sweet aisle and grab yourself a delicious bar of chocolate?

MARCUS: I don't want delicious chocolate, I wants me money.

BENNY: *(to Mr Hickling)* Do you have the ones with animals on them?

MR HICKLING: Aisle 5.

BENNY: 5.

MARCUS: Money first, we'll have chocolate to go.

BENNY: *(Folds arms)* Hello everyone, my name's Marcus and I decide how fast the world turns because I'm an unbelievable tit!

MARCUS: Was that supposed to be me?

BENNY: Well it isn't Lenny Henry is it?

JIMMY: If you'd said it more funnily, it could have had a whiff of Henry.

BENNY: You want some more of this?

BENNY moves his hands like a crab.

JIMMY: No sir!

BENNY: Less Lenny then.

MARCUS jumps once into the air and claps his hands.

MARCUS: Right, that's it.

BENNY: It is? Cool, let's be off then. We'll have a quick pit-stop at aisle…

MR HICKLING: 5!

BENNY: Aisle 5, yes, I'm famished.

BENNY turns to walk off and MARCUS grabs his collar and turns him back around.

MARCUS: Safe!

BENNY: I'm not going to be flattened by Dairy Milk am I?

MARCUS: Mr Hickling?

MR HICKLING: Yes.

MARCUS: Stand up.

BENNY: Saying that, some of those bars *are* pretty damn big. If a few fell on you…

MR HICKLING stands up.

MARCUS: Take me to the safe, *(raises gun)* now if you would.

BENNY: A glass and a half of whiplash!

MR HICKLING: If I must.

MARCUS: You really must.

MR HICKLING: Youth these days! What has the world come to and other slogans that are clichéd and mean very little!

MARTHA: You nasty, terrible, awful piece of filth.

MARCUS raises his eyebrows and BENNY leans in to him.

BENNY: She's talking to you.

MARCUS: She'll be talking to a bullet in a second.

BENNY: *(Makes a face)* That sounds like it would wreck.

MARCUS: Now Benny, you stay here and make sure that those two stay where *they* are. Mr Hickling and I are going on a little trip.

BENNY: Are you joking? Now's not the time to be gallivanting off on a trip.

MARCUS: To the safe!

BENNY: I know.

MARCUS: *(to Mr Hickling)* After you then.

BENNY opens the box where 'CAROL' is and takes it out.

BENNY: Wowzer! She's a looker isn't she?

MR HICKLING: Carol!

BENNY: Oh, so the little bit of a manager likes a bit of the sexy plastic does he?

MR HICKLING: Be careful with her; I gave her a facial recently.

BENNY: Hope it was make-up and not sperm!

A very uncomfortable and long pause.

MARCUS: *(Scratching head)* Well that's lowered the tone, thanks.

BENNY: You're quite welcome

MARCUS: Hickling, old chum, forward march.

He digs the gun into MR HICKLING's back and they exit.

BENNY: *(Shouting after them)* There's no gap to put anything through!

BENNY looks around, nervous. He doesn't really know what to do. He even smiles and waves at the two members of staff before putting 'CAROL' back in her box.

BENNY: The weather is a bit brisk isn't it? Very cold I think.

JIMMY: It's called snow mate.

MARTHA: Jimmy!

Another awkward moment follows. BENNY scratches his arse.

BENNY: You know what? I've got a right wedgie going on. I knew his disguise idea would prove to be uncomfortable.

MARTHA: When you've got the money, will you leave us alone?

JIMMY: I could be smoking weed and pulling actual birds right now, if I wasn't stacking shelves. I bet my PlayStation's gathering dust.

MARTHA: You won't hurt us will you? Go crazy or something?

BENNY: Do I look crazy to you? Of course I won't hurt anybody.

JIMMY coughs loudly.

BENNY: Any more than I have done already.

MARTHA: And the other one?

BENNY: Marcus? Shit – damn – bugger; I meant Bill, no Bill won't be doing anything either. Let's all be quiet shall we? Your voices are doing my head in.

MARTHA and JIMMY lay face down on the floor. BENNY paces with his hands in his pockets, whistling a tune. He walks to the curtain (SR) and picks up a packet of toilet rolls.

BENNY: *(to himself)* These should be free really. When you think about what they're for, you don't want to be shelling out too much.

He puts them down and walks/whistles to the opposite side of the stage. He reaches behind the curtain and picks up a tin of beans.

BENNY: Beans *are* my favourite. 'The best,' what's he on?

He puts the tin in his pocket after looking around to check nobody was watching.

BENNY: Nobody saw that.

He moves to centre-stage and looks down at the staff.

BENNY: Very quiet aren't you?

JIMMY: You told us to be quiet.

BENNY: You're not doing very well are you?

JIMMY: No!

BENNY: Don't worry I like to rebel too; look at where I am, great life so far. Everything's fine and dandy… Nothing wrong with me!

MARTHA: *(to JIMMY)* What's he thinking about?

JIMMY: Wanking!

MARTHA: Is that the new craze these days?

JIMMY: Nah, it's been going on for years!

THE HOST (played by Mr Hickling) pops his head out from behind the curtain (SR) from the same place as before. MARTHA and

JIMMY freeze and The Host makes a noise so BENNY looks at him.

BENNY: You again!

THE HOST: *(Mr Hickling)* Every single bit of me buddy. Are you feeling okay?

BENNY: Never felt as chipper as I do right now. Not bad in all.

THE HOST: *(Mr Hickling)* And what's the general feeling?

THE HOST walks tentatively toward BENNY, clenching his teeth.

BENNY: Better to get it over with they say.

THE HOST: *(Mr Hickling - Holding earpiece)* That's a go from Benny Watts, repeat, a go from Mr Watts.

TV THEME MUSIC

2 chairs are brought on by a runner and THE HOST and BENNY sit down. This happens DSL.

THE HOST: *(Mr Hickling)* So, hey there Benny, wow, thanks for joining us.

BENNY: Did I have a choice?

THE HOST: *(Mr Hickling - Laughs)* Nobody *chooses,* hey, let's talk about your childhood.

BENNY: Wasn't very interesting, do we have to talk about it?

THE HOST pulls out his prompt cards and scans through them.

THE HOST: *(Mr Hickling)* I didn't write the cards Benny, my assistant does that.

He laughs to the audience.

BENNY: I got scared from time to time. All the time you could say. I watched too many of those horror films. Bedtime was a nightmare; if it wasn't Freddy coming out of the walls, it was Jason under my bed. Don't even get me started on Candyman… I brushed my teeth in the kitchen, that's been haunting me for years.

THE HOST: *(Mr Hickling)* It says here that *(reads from card)* you never left the house if it looked like rain. Why was that?

BENNY shifts, uncomfortable in his chair.

BENNY: The drains… Pennywise!

THE HOST: *(Mr Hickling)* I see *(x5)*

THE HOST holds out a tissue to BENNY; it is waved away.

BENNY: I'm good.

THE HOST: *(Mr Hickling)* Let's go to the beginning. Back to where it all started, it being the beginning.

He laughs again to an audience that isn't there.

BENNY: Okay but my memory isn't an amazing one.

THE HOST: *(Mr Hickling - Holds earpiece)* Just make it up, we'll edit the truth in later.

BENNY: *(Deep breath)* I can only suppose that my childhood began when I was born…

We continue to watch BENNY pour his heart out to THE HOST who nods insincerely.

This is in silence now though as MARTHA gets the attention of JIMMY by shaking at his sleeve. They both look up at their 'minder' who has now frozen.

MARTHA: What do you think? He's not doing anything.

JIMMY: He looks pretty zoned out.

MARTHA: I'm not sure we should move, he may be testing us, ready to pounce.

JIMMY: Well I'm not going to lay here and do nothing, he's not even armed. I'm pretty sure I could take him. And with both of us, what chance does he have?

MARTHA: Jimmy, don't be a hero.

JIMMY: I'm not.

JIMMY jumps to his feet and extends his hand towards MARTHA.

JIMMY: *We* are!

She takes his hand and he helps her up. They stare at each other for an awkward moment.

JIMMY: You look beautiful in these artificial lights.

She blushes.

MARTHA: What a charmer, I never knew you had such hidden depths. Fancy kissing me?

JIMMY: There's no time for that. We've got a pair of unfunny clowns to make that little bit unfunny… er? Run and call the police.

MARTHA slowly walks off with her bad hip.

JIMMY: Now is the time, the time where a lowly teenage, minimum-waged shelf-stacker becomes a man. With a sixty-year old girlfriend apparently! Life can be weird, crap, but weird!

MARTHA re-enters and joins JIMMY.

MARTHA: It's done. I may walk slow and face one item per half hour, but I can dial a mean telephone.

JIMMY: You're like a living and breathing French & Saunders sketch. Has anybody ever told you…?

MARTHA: Cut the crap Jimmy, we'll talk sexy times at a later date. Right now I want you to grab a pair of melons.

JIMMY rushes toward her, hands ready to…

MARTHA: An actual pair of melons!

JIMMY immediately runs off, embarrassed. He comes back with a pair of melons and gives one to MARTHA.

JIMMY: Are we having a break? It's not even one in the morning.

MARTHA: No, we're going to show this wretched creature what happens when you try and use Naked Bargains for anything other than shopping.

JIMMY: Meaning?

MARTHA: That a best-laid plan can soon turn out to be a big pile of shite.

JIMMY: Got ya.

MARTHA: Ready?

JIMMY: After three.

MARTHA: Three.

They both raise their melons over BENNY's head.

JIMMY: Two.

They freeze and BENNY and THE HOST resume their interview.

THE HOST: *(Mr Hickling)* And horror films, the continuous watching and re-watching of them, were to blame?

BENNY: I suppose. I'd have much rather watched The Two Ronnie's Christmas specials, but, my brother thought it would toughen me up witnessing blood and guts again and again.

THE HOST: *(Mr Hickling)* I see *(x5)*

BENNY: And they never leave you do they? The images? They never leave your brain alone.

The sound of a baby crying begins.

BENNY: See what I mean?

THE HOST: *(Mr Hickling)* Everybody does Benny, maybe not as much as you.

Music plays in the background, nice, spooky music.

BENNY: I hear it.

THE HOST leans in and pats his knee.

THE HOST: *(Mr Hickling)* I do too. The thing is, what are *we* going to do about it?

BENNY: We've got to save the baby. The Candyman put him there.

THE HOST: *(Mr Hickling)* I believe you. What are you waiting for?

BENNY stands up and looks around the stage – the noise is coming from the stack of cereal and he goes to it.

BENNY: I'm not a wimp, I'm not a creep. I'm brave me, I am brave.

He begins to lift the cereal boxes down one by one.

BENNY: I'm coming, don't worry, I'll get to you.

BENNY gets on his hands and knees and crawls, disappearing into the boxes. They fall down over him and cover him. The crying stops

After a few moments, Benny re-appears, clutching a wrapped-up baby.

BENNY: There we are, I've got you, don't cry. Everything will be fine, you're safe.

He crawls back to where THE HOST is smiling in a more sinister way. The Host reaches down for the baby that BENNY holds up slowly. The Host takes the baby and pulls out a big bar of Dairy Milk; he beats Benny within an inch of his life. He exits.

BENNY, injured, pulls himself up to a standing position.

The music stops.

BENNY: I'm a hero.

MARTHA and JIMMY un-freeze.

MARTHA/JIMMY: One!

They both hit BENNY over the head with the melons. Benny drops to the floor.

JIMMY: One down… the other one to go.

MARTHA: Is he dead?

JIMMY: Not arsed me, shouldn't have been such a dick.

MR HICKLING and MARCUS re-enter. Marcus is holding a five-pound note in one hand, the gun in the other.

MARCUS: I've never heard of a safe that only contains a fiver. How does this place stay open?

MR HICKLING: We do our best.

MARCUS notices BENNY and grabs MR HICKLING around the throat, holding the gun to his head.

MARCUS: What the fuck's going on here?

JIMMY: We took matters into our own hands.

MARTHA: And by matters, we mean melons.

MARCUS: *(Upset)* Benny, Benjamin! He's my best friend you idiots, if he's dead I'll...

BENNY stirs.

MARCUS: Benny, you're okay?

BENNY: I saved the baby Marcus, I watched the film and I saved it. Not everyone has to kill something.

MARCUS: I might, if I don't leave here with more than a fiver.

BENNY: Look's good doesn't it, that gun? Looks like it could cause some real damage.

MARCUS: It will do if the banker doesn't up his offer.

BENNY: You can't tell the difference. I couldn't tell... looks like the real thing to me.

MARCUS: *(Pause)* The *real* thing.

BENNY: *(Coughs – dying)* Yep.

MARCUS: It is real, you ordered it from that gun shop remember? It was a secret gun shop only we knew about.

BENNY: Marcus, who do you think I am, Scarface?

MARCUS: Maybe.

BENNY: It's a replica, not even that. It's from the Whitby Joke Shop. Good though isn't it?

MARCUS: *(Pause)* It's… it's a *gun.*

BENNY: Thanks for being my best friend Marcus. I bloody love you, did you know that? Of course you didn't, friends rarely say that to each other … *(deep breath)* they should though… you never know when it's going to be your last…

BENNY dies.

We hear police sirens

Pause – MARCUS let's go of MR HICKLING who runs to MARTHA and JIMMY.

MARCUS: *(Confused)* This was a joke!

He pulls the trigger and nothing happens. Lights fade. END.

For Your Displeasure Plays

The Leather Dinner Party

Written by Alan Pickthall 2008

Performed at the Edinburgh Fringe Festival 2009

CAST OF PERVERTS

Hosts of the party;

PETER MISTAKE

GILLIAN MISTAKE

A couple, new to the neighbourhood;

CLIVE BUMS

MARY BUMS

A small table centre-stage – PETER MISTAKE enters holding a bowl of cherries. He circles the table, eyeing up both the table and the bowl in his hands. He moves his hand, gesturing the width of the table, measuring it. He stops and puts the cherries down, moves back, looks down and picks them back up.
GILLIAN MISTAKE enters, holding a plate of sandwiches. They are very well-spoken.

PETER: Cherries?

GILLIAN: *(Nodding)* Sandwiches.

They place their plate or bowl down from each side of the table, look up at each other, then down and swap plates/bowl to the opposite side of the table. They look up at each other.

PETER: I love you.

GILLIAN: I love you.

They walk backwards off-stage, slowly, gazing at each other, eye contact held. Off for a brief moment – they soon return and enter, standing either side of the stage holding a fresh set of plates (Peter (R) – Gillian (L)) this time they say the names of the foods in a more sensuous manner. Peter picks up a crabstick from his plate and takes off the wrapper using one hand.

PETER: *(Looking at her)* Crab… stick!

He throws it in his mouth and licks each finger afterwards. Gillian has a basket of fruit and picks up a banana, peeling it.

GILLIAN: Banana.

She bites a chunk off and eats it, Peter shivers. They bring the food to the table, look down and immediately pass each other the food, then place them down.

PETER: I bloody love you.

GILLIAN: I love you more than I love myself.

They both run off and return quicker than before. Peter picks some crisps off a plate and holds them, his palm out-stretched. He seems to be very proud of them for some reason.

PETER: Crisps!

He closes his hand and crushes them; he places the remains in his dressing gown pocket – shivering as he does so. Gillian holds a bar of chocolate which she strips of its wrapper. She does this seductively, as she would no doubt strip a man of his clothing.

GILLIAN: Chocolate?

She puts one end into her mouth and lightly bites down, she walks centre-stage, in front of the table and Peter meets her. He bites the opposite end – they both bite down, a chunk off each and the remainder falls to the floor. Whilst chewing…

PETER: Dark would be better.

GILLIAN: Dark *would* be better.

PETER / GILLIAN: I love you.

Pause.

PETER / GILLIAN: I love you more.

Peter holds a hand over her mouth. She is trying to profess her love whilst being gagged with his hand.

PETER: I think you'll find I love you so much more than your sister.

He takes hand away, she gasps for air, slightly composes herself.

GILLIAN: I want to murder you sexily, make love to the body – bonk you back to life and then we can have children.

Peter shivers in a disgusted way and steps forward of her. His previous mood is now ruined.

PETER: Why? Why now? I was feeling all erotic but this incessant talk of children spoils everything, my erections nowhere to be found.

GILLIAN: Darling don't be a kettle; I don't have many friends around here, that's what tonight is for. If I had children though, they could keep me company – I could be friends with our seed!

PETER: Yes, I am glad we're having this party – a chance to meet the new neighbours. They could be your new friends.

GILLIAN: Parties are good.

PETER: They are indeed. I hope we have things in common; I just loathe people who are different.

He says different with a tremble of the lip.

GILLIAN: Oh I remember them talking like us, they seem to have proper tongues!

PETER: Fantastic, when you invited them, did they sound a bit kinky at all?

GILLIAN: Oh yes, she wore lace and wore a *tweed* jacket – I practically had a threesome right there in the post office.

PETER: *(Miming)* I like to lick the envelope.

Gillian immediately walks forward to meet him and puts a hand on his shoulder. She gives it a little squeeze.

GILLIAN: I'll go get one from the bureau!

She starts to walk off but is stopped dead by the sound of the doorbell. The sound of it causes her to jump and turn.

PETER: There's no time *(brushes her hand away)* they're already here.

GILLIAN: How do I look?

PETER: *(Holds her hand)* Magnificent – how do I look?

GILLIAN: *(She lifts his hand to eye level)* Married!

They smile at each other

PETER: Chortle.

GILLIAN: Snigger.

They move toward each other. The doorbell rings again. Peter shouts, head facing off-stage.

PETER: Henry? *(Louder)* Henry!

GILLIAN: Who is Henry?

PETER: The butler.

GILLIAN: Darling, we don't have a butler.

PETER: Why ever not?

GILLIAN: He died months ago!

Doorbell sounds again and Gillian jumps.

PETER: Be a dear and answer the door.

GILLIAN: *(Confused)* You threw the antlers out, you said they were mucky.

PETER: Answer it as yourself then.

GILLIAN: I can't answer it, I'm a *woman*.

PETER: It's because you're a woman I must insist you answer it!

GILLIAN: I won't pretend I didn't hear that, because I did. But let it be known my earrings are falling apart and your testicles would look mighty nice adorning my wifely lobes.

PETER: What are you implying?

GILLIAN: You loosing particulars and me gaining accessories.

PETER: Just answer the door.

She leaves to answer the door – he inspects the table. He talks to himself.

PETER: And I will wait in the dining area to greet our new friends to a party… a party of fun, frolics and fancy-free fuddle-dum.

Gillian returns to the side of the stage – this time accompanied with CLIVE and MARY BUMS. Peter continues unwittingly.

PETER: In my naughty silky dressing gown. Oh gosh what a riddle you are gown *(he starts caressing it)* you are there to warm me I know, yet you are just asking to be peeled off.

He exposes his shoulder.

GILLIAN: Peter darling?

Peter spins around to face them.

PETER: What is it?

He notices they are staring at his shoulder and pulls the gown up over it once more.

GILLIAN: These are our new neighbours.

Clive and Mary step forward. They both look very nervous but are trying their very hardest to smile.

CLIVE: My name's Clive Bums and this is my wife Mary.

MARY: I'm called that.

They all shake hands.

PETER: Mr Bums, it's good to meet you… and you Mrs Bums.

He takes her hand of Mary and kisses it. He then looks at each finger, stopping at the middle finger and sucks it, nothing is said.

PETER: Cherry nail varnish? The classic edition I'm sure.

MARY: I don't know about that but thank you very much.

PETER: The pleasure is all mine and could possibly be all yours very soon.

Gillian looks at him from over Mary's shoulder – she mouths 'Not now' at him. Clive and Mary look more nervous.

GILLIAN: Why don't I take the coats?

She goes about taking the coats off of Mary and Clive who are formally dressed for a dinner party, nice dress and hat for Mary, Clive in a well-laundered suit.
Mary notices that the other couple are wearing dressing gowns.

MARY: I'm sorry, are we early? It's just that you don't seem to be particularly ready; I feel we've interrupted you. Should we leave?

PETER: Oh no, that would be simply dreadful.

GILLIAN: I can't think of anything worse than for you to leave.

PETER: Apart from death.

GILLIAN: Apart from death, that's right I forgot about that. Other than that, don't go!

CLIVE: *(Unsure)* Then we shall stay and enjoy your company – however you choose to dress in your household is completely your choice *(to Mary)*. Though it didn't say anything about it being a slumber party did it?

Clive and Mary laugh whilst Peter and Gillian look at each other, shrugging off an outburst. Gillian, forcing a subject change, gestures towards the table and all the items on top of it.

GILLIAN: Won't you have a nibble from the table?

MARY: Thank you that would be lovely.

They all walk to the table – Mary and Clive behind it, Peter and Gillian either side of it.

MARY: It's a nice spread isn't it Clive?

CLIVE: It is nice, more of a wipe than a spread; a slight graze of food.

PETER: It's all of the highest quality, the crisps are imported I believe.

Clive holds up a crab stick in disgust.

CLIVE: I've no doubt. Pre-packaged food needs to be held at an arm's length.

Peter gives Gillian a nod – 'tis a nod of 'okay – let's do this!

GILLIAN: Did you find a parking space? I really should have gotten Peter to move some of the cars, gosh; we have so many don't we?

PETER: Yes, it's amazing we keep track of all the keys, we have so many cars.

MARY: We didn't drive, we only live next door.

CLIVE: We don't actually own a car; we've gone 'green'. Mary and I are always doing a bit to save the planet. There is only one after all and what a shame it would be to ruin it so soon.

PETER: My dear Gillian once used a carrier bag three times to accompany her on different shopping trips – the same bag!

CLIVE: That's hardly going to save the world my good sir. Mary and I don't boil the kettle for endless cups of tea; we just imagine that we are drinking scolding hot tea! We even have actions don't we Mary?

MARY: Yes.

CLIVE: Come on Mary, what do we do when we imagine something is hot?

Mary performs a feeble action as if she has drunk something hot.

CLIVE: Yes use our imaginations to stay green – it's really not very nice!

MARY: Yes, I don't like that.

CLIVE: Shush Mary! Perhaps we should leave after all?

Clive stands up, Gillian gently forces him to sit down again.

GILLIAN: I wouldn't hear of it.

She runs to the doorway and blocks it.

GILLIAN: I must insist you stay.

CLIVE: You don't seem ready to 'host' that's all.

GILLIAN: We are, don't worry, your right on time.

CLIVE: Mary does say I have a knack for punctuality. Don't you Mary?

MARY: Yes, I've said that.

GILLIAN: *(Moving forward from door)* My husband is frightfully punctual.

PETER: Oh, frightfully so.

GILLIAN: Indeed, remember when you turned up to that conference three years early?

PETER: I'm still there in fact.

They both laugh like sods!

MARY: You've been to a conference haven't you Clive?

CLIVE: I have Mary, a Conservative Party conference…

Peter spits at him – it hits his jacket, everyone stares, except Peter who just stares at the spit.

PETER: Sorry, force of habit.

CLIVE: Anyway I shook hands with many an MP.

PETER: MP? Pffh!

CLIVE: I'm sorry, is there a problem?

PETER: Oh no, not at all. *(Smirks)*

CLIVE: What party do you support?

PETER: Not the conservatives that's for sure.

CLIVE: Who then?

PETER: The BN…

He stops himself.

GILLIAN: Bien… we support the French! Our neighbours they are, and we like to support our neighbours in any way we can.

PETER: Cupping balls!

Gillian looks at Peter and drools, mops it up and changes the subject.

GILLIAN: How much does it pay to be a Conservative?

CLIVE: Well, nothing – I was there as a supporter… supporting.

MARY: Like a Wonder-Bra, he's very supportive is my Clive. He'd do anything for anyone, as long as they speak proper!

PETER: Gosh, it's like looking in a mirror, luckily we have a massive income, don't we Gillian?

GILLIAN: Very true that statement you just made was, and speaking of statements.

She walks to the table and picks up some napkins.

GILLIAN: You'll notice that your napkins for this evening are made using our old bank statements. Talk about being green they say.

PETER: But don't look at them, I'd feel ever so big-headed if you were to chance a peek.

CLIVE: I wouldn't dream of it.

MARY: Clive and I don't mind people knowing how much we earn, as we do give a substantial amount to a variety of charities.

Gillian confronts her so the two are face to face.

GILLIAN: Really? Do tell.

MARY: *(Grasping for words)* Well the RSPCA and the NSPCC for starters.

GILLIAN: *(Sarcastic)* That is very good of you.

PETER: Though we made a pact to never have children in the first place, therefore there's zero chance of abuse ever even occurring.

GILLIAN: *(To Mary)* I've made no such pact!

PETER: *(Clicks fingers)* Henry! I take it your thirsty?

Clive and Mary nod.

PETER: Drinky-poo's Henry!

Gillian walks to Peter and puts both hands on his shoulders, looking at him deep in the eyes.

GILLIAN: No butler.

PETER: Ah, never a truer word spoken. Would you then get our hosts a drink?

GILLIAN: There our guests Peter.

PETER: Whom?

GILLIAN: They are the guests – we, are the hosts!

PETER: Oh so I've always had it the wrong way round all these years?

GILLIAN: I think!

PETER: That's why my parties always have an air of ill-feeling. *(Turns to Clive and Mary)* I'm very expectant, that's my downfall.

CLIVE: Its okay actually, Mary doesn't drink.

GILLIAN: What? Never ever? How does she function?

PETER: That's proper shish!

CLIVE: No not at all, Mary was an alcoholic for five years before just last week, isn't that correct Mary?

MARY: Oh yes, I did like a glass of wine.

CLIVE: Come on Mary, come on, you can tell Daddy.

Peter and Gillian hold hands and watch.

MARY: A vat, a vat of wine, I actually filled the bathtub with merlot and bathed in grapes.

CLIVE: And how bad did it get?

MARY: I wouldn't get out till the bath was empty.

CLIVE: *(To P & G)* Sometimes I wouldn't see her for days! *(Back to M)* And what would you eventually resemble?

MARY: *(Eyes wide)* A big raisin.

CLIVE: A big raisin! That's right; you're doing ever so well.

He kisses Mary on the hand.

PETER: You hang in there.

GILLIAN: Don't ever give up on being you.

MARY: Thank you.

GILLIAN: Perhaps she would like a water?

CLIVE: I'm sure she would. Mary?

MARY: *(Looks off-stage)* Water.

CLIVE: I'd have an apple juice.

GILLIAN: Good choice, I'll just venture to the orchard out back – we have many bushels don't we Peter?

Gillian walks off.

PETER: We eat so many apples; it's a really productive side-business actually.

CLIVE: You're self-employed?

PETER: Of course, I wouldn't dream of having a boss – I answer only to myself and even then there are disagreements. No there isn't! Yes there is! Why don't you both take a seat?

Mary and Clive sit – Gillian re-enters with a small carton of apple juice and a glass of water. She gives them to the couple – Clive inspects his carton.

CLIVE: I thought you had an orchard?

GILLIAN: A big one, it needs trimming.

CLIVE: Pardon?

GILLIAN: The carton? It's a habit I have.

PETER: Gillian likes to dissolve class prejudice, to avoid any misunderstandings she extracts the essence from the apple…

GILLIAN: From the orchard!

PETER: That's right and pours the apple essence extract into a Del Monte carton…

GILLIAN: Or an Um Bongo!

PETER: Or that, quite, it's purely to put any person less-privileged than ourselves at ease.

CLIVE: That's insane.

PETER: It's simply so that they can drink from something that they feel comfortable with.

GILLIAN: We could hardly serve juice from the ornate vases we usually sip from.

Peter and Gillian laugh.

CLIVE: I'm not sure if that's not actually adding to the class system problem? You know, making it more apparent, more visible?

GILLIAN: I think it's the way God would want it.

MARY: I'm feeling a little hot – is your heating on?

Peter and Gillian look at each other.

PETER: Oh my, your right it is rather hot, isn't it darling?

GILLIAN: Perhaps a tad too hot.

PETER: I'm sweating.

GILLIAN: Whereabouts?

PETER: You can't imagine.

GILLIAN: More water Mary?

MARY: I don't know.

GILLIAN: Well you will let me know if Mr Thirst comes a knocking on your bladder won't you?

MARY: Oh he knocks alright!

CLIVE: Mary has a weak bladder. Has done ever since she was kicked in the fanny by a young hooligan. Isn't that right Mary?

MARY: *(Nodding)* I've a moist gusset as we speak.

PETER: I feel we should get to know each other a little better. You are new to the neighbourhood after all.

CLIVE: What do you want to know?

Gillian sits down.

GILLIAN: Everything.

Peter sits – all four are now seated.

PETER: Not actually *everything*, some things are better left to the imagination. Wouldn't you agree dearest?

GILLIAN: *(Casually)* Not at all.

CLIVE: I was born in a rural village if I remember correctly, a market town.

PETER: And when did you meet your lovely wife?

GILLIAN: Nail her quickly did you?

CLIVE: Excuse me?

GILLIAN: How quickly did you marry?

CLIVE: We courted for a few months, I asked her father if I could propose and…

GILLIAN: Over a washing machine *(to Peter)* that's how I imagine it… *(to Clive)* they do have a certain motion that is good for more than washing.

PETER: I like the hair dryer – nice and warm on my…

CLIVE: Perhaps you should tell us how you two met.

PETER: Certainly. Ours was a meeting of sorts, one that you could only find in the pages of Dickens.

GILLIAN: I've read that book! Me and my husband like literature.

MARY: Any favourites?

GILLIAN: No we're very open-minded.

PETER: And open-mouthed.

They both laugh loudly

GILLIAN: Yes he was accidentally a dentist at one point, when we first gazed into each other's eyeballs.

They both start to speak even more 'posh.'

PETER: Doth I would forsooth see her anon.

CLIVE: I don't follow.

GILLIAN: I made many appointments even though my tooth's were in tippity top condition. These were the yonder days when I would wear semi-revealing garments and he would put his little mirror inside me.

PETER: That isn't a euphemism – well not at first it wasn't.

GILLIAN: We were married before supper.

MARY: Do you knit?

CLIVE: *(Shouting)* Mary! How rude.

MARY: Sorry.

CLIVE: Better! Do you knit?

GILLIAN: Once. It hurt.

PETER: We have so many interests that occupy our time – we like to keep things interesting, in all rooms, don't we?

GILLIAN: Yes.

MARY: I've always wanted to spice things up in a certain room.

Peter stands up, suddenly very interested.

PETER: Really?

CLIVE: I've never heard any complaints.

MARY: That's because you don't listen to me.

CLIVE: My everything, you know why that is don't you?

MARY: Why?

CLIVE/PETER: Because you're a woman!

Clive and Peter look at each other, pause, smile and sigh – they've found like-mindedness.

PETER: Alcohol Clive?

CLIVE: Fill my boots Peter.

He pours him a gigantic drink from the table. The two women sit exactly like each other – arms/legs crossed.

CLIVE: I'm starting to feel comfortable here Mary.

Peter slowly exposes his shoulder.

MARY: That's good news.

CLIVE: Yes, not so comfortable I want to play strip chequers and not wash my hands after urinating, but comfy nonetheless.

Peter pulls his robe up over his shoulder again. He taps Gillian on her shoulder and whispers something in her ear.

GILLIAN: Actually on the subject of games – perhaps we should play something, any suggestions?

PETER: Too many to mention.

MARY: How about charades?

GILLIAN: *(Makes a face)* Not a believer in charades I'm afraid, there's too much thinking involved?

PETER: It reminds me of prison.

CLIVE: What would you say to a game of chess?

PETER: I'd say fuck you chess and close the door behind you.'

GILLIAN: The wit! That's why I married you; I knew there was a reason.

CLIVE: What game would you like to play?

GILLIAN: I don't know.

She leans over him, revealing a leg; Clive looks at it with both worry and interest.

GILLIAN: I like games that are a little more physically demanding.

Peter walks over to Mary and twirls the tassels of his gown in her face.

PETER: Yes, I'm a firm believer in the physical games.

MARY: Like tennis?

PETER: That could be incorporated somehow I suppose.

CLIVE: I'm confused – what's happening at this point?

GILLIAN: What do you want to happen?

CLIVE: I'd rather a glass of sherry right now!

GILLIAN: *(Like encouraging a child)* That's good, have another drink, that will fit this evening perfectly.

PETER: I know what would also be perfect right now.

MARY: What?

PETER: Music.

GILLIAN: Bravo Peter dear, that will slow things down somewhat; we are moving a little fast.

She runs off-stage left and comes back on with an LP, she runs off-stage the other side and we hear the motion of her doing something that has sounds.

Piano music begins to play, really rather nice and the three on stage nod along, enjoying it. Gillian returns.

CLIVE: That's really rather nice, what is it?

PETER: Music.

Gillian holds up the LP cover, white sleeve with black writing – it reads…

GILLIAN: 'Bonk' by 'Seduction in the Minor Key'. Very rare this record, rarely spectacular music – ideal for dinner parties such as what you're experiencing.

MARY: I used to play the piano, ever since I was a child. But as I grew up my talent ceased to exist due to my overbearing father who always…

Clive stops her with a hand on her shoulder.

CLIVE: Boring Mary, yawn!

PETER: I thought it was interesting, please continue Mary.

CLIVE: I'll speak for her if you don't mind?

PETER: I do mind. I find your wife interesting and possibly very slutty!

CLIVE: What was that?

PETER: *(Anxious)* She's sloppy, dripped food all over her blouse – get the woman a bib man!

GILLIAN: Let's all drink shall we? New neighbours forward slash friends don't fall out at their very first dinner party. We are all adults, well-bred, respectful and resentful of the lower.

They all drink, there is an uncomfortable silence.
The music suddenly changes and in the midst of the piano come groans and moans of sexual proportions. A voice whispers "Bonk" inappropriately.
Gillian and Peter look at the other two, gauging reaction. Clive and Mary look flabbergasted.

CLIVE: I'm not sure this is my cup of tea. And forgive me if I'm wrong but are those subliminal yelps I can hear?

PETER: I like to call them groans.

GILLIAN: I can't hear a thing. Perhaps Clive, you've demonstrated your temperament tonight.

CLIVE: Whatever do you mean?

GILLIAN: The mind hears what it wants to hear, don't fight its capability Clive; embrace the yelps.

PETER: Groans!

GILLIAN: *Moans* is my preferred description. If music be the food of love, bend me over and give me what for!

Gillian and Peter dance to the music. They slap each other twice each.

Mary stands up and screams…

MARY: Turn it off, please turn it off.

The music stops suddenly leaving one singular moan without piano. Peter and Gillian look to see why the music has been turned off with everyone present on-stage.

PETER: *(Confused)* Henry?

CLIVE: I'm sorry for that outburst, Mary how could you? And in the company of our new friends? Shame on you – a curse on all your houses!

GILLIAN: We're… your… friends?

CLIVE: Yes whatever you want; friends.

PETER: You know what this means sugar minge?

GILLIAN: I do indeedy Jesus penis. Now you are our friends, we can have the dinner party we've wanted since you two stepped through the door.

PETER: Cock candles!

GILLIAN: That's what we need Peter, the cock candles.

CLIVE: What the hell are those?

PETER: The clues in the name really.

GILLIAN: They're fantastic.

PETER: They ejaculate light upon us – they're ideal.

Gillian runs off and comes back on with two candles, she puts them on the table and is about to light them.

MARY: I have a phobia of fire.

CLIVE: Oh Mary, you are a twat.

PETER: Interesting, I have a phobia of clothing.

GILLIAN: *(Puts hand up)* I share that phobia!

MARY: Ever since I was a child.

GILLIAN: Don't worry, we'll leave it for now and light them later.

Peter folds arms and tuts like a child – Gillian notices this and walks toward him.

GILLIAN: There there you!

She twists his nipple through his gown and he smiles again.

CLIVE: Why don't you serve dinner?

MARY: I'm famished.

CLIVE: We all are Mary; we all are!

Gillian and Peter look at each other, worried.

PETER: Dinner? What is that?

GILLIAN: A small country?

PETER: Probably.

CLIVE: You do have a meal prepared for tonight?

Gillian points to the table.

CLIVE: Is that it? When we were in the post office you said there was a three-course meal.

GILLIAN: You can eat… crabsticks, sandwiches *(pause)* and crisps.

CLIVE: Did you mistake us for five year olds?

PETER: I think we should forget about the food for now.

PETER / GILLIAN: Enter into our world.

Mary and Clive are sat down – Peter and Gillian stand either side of them.
They undo their dressing gowns and drop them to the floor. They both wear black leather and PVC bondage gear.

PETER: Hello friends.

GILLIAN: Join us.

CLIVE / MARY: Oh my God!

There is a huge pause – Gillian and Peter stand in weird poses, like statues.

PETER: Well, what do you think?

GILLIAN: Aren't we divine?

Peter walks to Mary and sits on her lap.

PETER: You look worried Mary. Don't be! After tonight you'll only ever want to wear wipe clean. For the rest of your life.

Gillian walks to Clive and sits on his lap.

GILLIAN: Life is so much noisier when you wrap yourself up in sturdy bin bags.

CLIVE: I didn't expect this.

MARY: They're like cartoons!

PETER: Would you like to spank me?

MARY: *(To Clive)* Would I?

CLIVE: Go on then.

Peter stands, facing the audience, bends over slightly and Mary lightly taps his behind.

PETER: Now Mary – you can do better than that.

She does it again, harder this time, Peter enjoys it but we see he is in pain.

PETER: *(Turns and winks at her)* Not your first time is it? *(To Clive)* You've a good wife there Mr Bums.

Peter sits down on her lap again – Gillian lifts a foot and puts it on the chair between Clive's legs.

GILLIAN: Do you like shoes Clive?

CLIVE: I've worn shoes yes!

GILLIAN: Do you write letter?

CLIVE: Not really – I use e-mail.

GILLIAN: Do you know anyone who has a birthday?

CLIVE: Yes.

GILLIAN: And do you wish them a happy birthday Clive?

CLIVE: Where is this going?

GILLIAN: *(Commanding)* Do you?

CLIVE: I do.

GILLIAN: You know the part where you have to seal the envelope?

CLIVE: I'm not licking your shoes!

She puts her foot on the floor.

GILLIAN: Fine, but Mary spanked my husband, so that means you're a prude, you'll be the talk of the town, 'Prude' they will shout, 'Look at that prude'.

PETER: Gillian, he's not ready, leave him alone. I'd expect better from you.

GILLIAN: I'd expect better from less-privileged individuals.

Clive and Mary now talk with regional accents. Not only have accents changed, Clive and Mary move differently and their real faces have been revealed.

CLIVE: How is all of this privileged?

Gillian and Peter are speechless, they stand together and Clive pushes into the middle of them.

GILLIAN: Did you just speak different?

PETER: He did, I heard, he spoke common.

GILLIAN: And in our house? Bugger me.

CLIVE: That's right, I did and I do. God I can't take any more of that fake pomposity. *(Mimicking posh voices)* 'We have a billion cars / we've been to the moon / we have diamonds for eyes!'

GILLIAN: What a fabulous idea.

PETER: I wish I had diamonds for eyes.

MARY: I want to leave, I'm not happy anymore. This dinner party is shit.

GILLIAN: *(Really offended)* How could you say that to me, about my dinner party? And with those vocal chords!

She cries for a few seconds then composes herself.

PETER: I'm sure I'm bleeding just because you're right there.

Mary gets up and heads for the door which Clive blocks.

CLIVE: Don't Mary; just hang on a couple of minutes.

PETER: I'm sorry Clive but common folk like you two shouldn't be in the presence of this mammoth concoction I'm wearing.

CLIVE: It's a monstrosity, you can keep it mate.

He walks to the table and grabs and eats a handful of crisps. He uses a napkin to wipe his mouth and hands and slowly unfolds it, looking at it carefully.

GILLIAN: We can no longer be friends, which Peter means we must now have children, due to the fact that your voices disgust me.

PETER: I hope you're pleased with yourselves; I only wanted a party with a bit of slap and tickle; now I must have children! Leave my house!

MARY: We're going you whore!

GILLIAN: Did you hear that Peter? She called me a whore.

PETER: Delightful; perhaps she's coming round.

CLIVE: I think I am actually.

PETER / GILLIAN: You are?

MARY: Are you?

CLIVE: I am.

PETER: But you're a Conservative.

GILLIAN: *(Exaggerated common voice)* And talk like this!

CLIVE: I know but, can't we set aside our differences.

GILLIAN: No.

CLIVE: Just for tonight? Just one little orgy?

PETER: Yes.

GILLIAN: But…

PETER: Let's see what happens.

GILLIAN: Shall I put the music back on?

MARY: No.

CLIVE: Show me. Show me what you like to do?

PETER: I don't want to now, I feel like I'm on display.

GILLIAN: What would you like to see?

Clive looks at Mary, she looks back; they turn to the couple.

CLIVE / MARY: Everything...

Lights down. The music 'Bonk' comes on again.

Lights up – Peter and Gillian are tied to two chairs back to back, Gillian has a bag on her head and mumbles from now on when speaking, she has been drugged. The table is gone.

PETER: Oh how silly have we been?

GILLIAN: Very!

PETER: It looked promising at first, when he went and got a cucumber out of the fridge which he...

GILLIAN: Ow!

PETER: Yes, he beat you with it, I know.

Gillian cries hysterically.

PETER: Don't cry sugar minge, somebody is bound to find us soon.

He looks off-stage.

PETER: Oh no, they've taken our golden garden gnomes as well. I mean, steal the cars but leave the gnomes for heavens. This is the world we live in Gillian – a world where two of God's children (that's me and you of course) are made to suffer the cards dealt by folk who don't even know how to enjoy themselves. Perhaps we should give up trying to make friends with people who don't understand us, we know what feels good; we know that pain sometimes equals pleasure.

GILLIAN: Not now.

PETER: Yes not now… though I did have an erection when he stamped on a crab stick. It's gone now though.

He looks off-stage.

PETER: Oh no, they've took the garden as well. Heathens, not content with clearing the house they've stolen the garden. Honestly they're just tying it on the roof of the van now. Somebody will come though; they always do… *(Pause and then shouting)* Henry! Henry, help us. It's no use… he's not real!

Gillian cries and says something unintelligible.

PETER: I know sperm blossom… I bloody love you too!

Lights fade down and the last thing we see is Peter trying to wriggle free.

THE END

For Your Displeasure Plays

Crow's Feet

Written by Alan Pickthall 2012

Characters

Hilda

Edna

Agatha

A Gasman

A lovely tablecloth sits on top of the table. There is a vase of dead flowers sitting in the centre and a few small piles of books are laid around. There are also small piles of books on the floor near the legs of the table.
Three china cups are arranged.
HILDA PAGE enters SR and is singing something quite inaudible; sounds nice though and eventually we hear it...

HILDA: 'I'm in the mood, for reading a book or two. Won't you lick your fingers and join me in my fictional paradise?'

She looks at the table and specifically at the flowers.

HILDA puts on her glasses, smiles at the audience and looks at the flowers on her table. The smile fades slowly.

HILDA: *(Disgusted)* What hideous flowers. Who the flaming heck put *them* there? Oh it was me... *(Slaps her own face)* Silly Hilda, you're a daft bugger if you think you'll ever win 1st prize, how I hate them!

She takes the flowers out of the vase, snapping them in two. Her anger gets the better of her and she shakes the teapot. She looks at the biscuits, her hands still on the teapot.

HILDA: And you biscuits can piss off as well.

HILDA smashes most of the biscuits with her fist.

HILDA: *(To audience)* They were laughing at me they were!

She looks at the biscuits and picks one up to show the audience.

HILDA: It really doesn't help that they all have smiley faces upon their delicious fronts.

She puts the biscuit down, aims her fist and smashes it with three hits.

HILDA: Who's smiling now? *(Listens for a reaction)* That's correct my nemesis, none of you are; you're all crumbs you lot. You hear me? Crumbs!

EDNA and AGATHA enter stage-right, stand still and look at her. These two are of the same, older age as Hilda is. They look quite embarrassed.

EDNA: Hilda?

AGATHA: Hilda dear, what on earth is the matter?

HILDA stands up and looks very calm.

HILDA: Terry it was, I think his name was Terry.

AGATHA whispers into EDNA'S ear.

AGATHA: Oh no, mysterious husband alert!

EDNA: It seems so yes.

AGATHA: A change of subject?

EDNA: Quick-sharpish I'd say.

They both face HILDA and with exaggerated smiles and open arms, they approach her, both planting a kiss on either side of face.
EDNA is stood on the left of Hilda and AGATHA stands on the right.

AGATHA: I made a most scrumptious cake the other day. It was to die for, wasn't it Edna?

EDNA: Yes Agatha, to die for. I nearly did too; choked on a chunk of marzipan! Very dangerous but ultimately delicious marzipan is.

AGATHA: It's true, I had to call a neighbour to do one of those manoeuvres that people do nowadays.

HILDA: Did you now?

AGATHA: It worked a treat. You couldn't tell what was carpet and what was marzipan.

AGATHA and EDNA laugh.

AGATHA: Imagine having a marzipan carpet all the way through your house.

EDNA: Your curtains made from liquorice?

AGATHA: Indeed; a chocolate table and a toffee toilet, my, how would one live?

EDNA: Very obese I would imagine.

They laugh again. EDNA becomes embarrassed.

EDNA: I still feel ever so embarrassed about that Agatha. Making a complete 'to do' of myself.

AGATHA: Please Edna, don't mention it again. The sucker-up of dust that I plug in swallowed whole the last sugary clump this morning; all's well.

EDNA: That ends well; oh I do love a good Shakespeare! Hilda, tell us the Bard will be the first book of our soon to be esteemed book club?

HILDA: Let me see… *(she thinks)* I'm afraid that I haven't decided on our first book yet. I thought it best to wait for you both so that we could decide as a group.

AGATHA and EDNA both sit down on either side of HILDA who they each lay a hand on and drag down to a sitting position. Agatha takes out a book from her handbag.

AGATHA: I would very much like to nominate this book for our first read.

HILDA: That's a cookery book Agatha.

EDNA: Lovely idea, what's it about?

AGATHA: It's about recipes!

EDNA: I like it; tell me more.

AGATHA: Pies and pastries…

HILDA: As much as I appreciate the originality Agatha, I do *not* think that a cookery book will provide ample opportunity for discussion and debate.

AGATHA: Of course it would.

HILDA: How would it?

AGATHA: We could discuss the ingredients and debate their relevance to the dish, including our own methods and ingredient substitutions when cooking savoury and sweet treats.

EDNA: *(Hand up)* I vote cookery book!

HILDA: We're not voting yet Edna.

EDNA puts her hand down, then rummages in her own bag.

AGATHA: I did try Hilda; you can't say that I haven't given it a thought.

HILDA: That is true. Well done for doing so.

EDNA removes a copy of OK magazine and holds it up in presentation, waiting for HILDA to notice.

HILDA: If we are serious about this book club becoming an annual event, we *must* be serious about the reading matter also.

EDNA lowers her magazine and subtlety places it back inside her bag.

AGATHA: Have you any possibilities in your mind Hilda? I think that perhaps you should decide because it's your house, the base for the club, so you should have final say.

HILDA: I suppose we could take it in turns. I mean rotate the decision; every three years we each get to decide the book to read?

AGATHA: Yes, that's a marvellous idea. Don't you think so Edna?

EDNA: *(A bit moody)* I suppose that would be a good idea.

AGATHA: What was that dear? I'm not as young as I was, I can't hear you very well.

EDNA: *(Shouts)* OKAY, WHATEVER, THAT'S FINE BY ME!

AGATHA: Are you trying to deafen me? I'm not as young as I once was. My ear drums popped just now. Hilda did yours?

HILDA: Oh, I lost my ear drums a long time ago.

AGATHA: Probably in a drawer somewhere; everyone's got one.

HILDA: I'll choose the book then.

EDNA: You do that.

HILDA: I will do Edna.

EDNA: Oh goody.

HILDA: Are you being a bit of a bottom Edna?

EDNA: Yes. *(She blows a raspberry)*

HILDA: Just so we're clear with each other.

AGATHA has a finger in her left ear and has turned away from her friends.

AGATHA: My little ear drum… inside my ear, poor little thing. It feels like The Beatles have reformed inside of my head!

EDNA: I do sometimes get the most terrible pounding in between my ears. Sometimes sounds like little Timmy Hendrix has risen from the grave.

HILDA: You mean Jimmi dear…

EDNA: No, *Timmy Hendrix.*

HILDA: But you mean Jimmi Hendrix I'm sure.

EDNA: *(Offended)* It's my headache Hilda. So if it sounds like little Timmy Hendrix riffing some licks, then little Timmy Hendrix it is. I don't tell you how your illnesses sound do I?

HILDA is about to come back with something but we see her change her mind.

HILDA: So, back to the decision of what book to read. I don't know about you both but there are some classics that have passed me by these last few decades. Some of which I would very much like to read and now have reason to, before I knock over the dreaded bucket with a misplaced foot.

EDNA: Kick the bucket?

HILDA: No, knock it over with a misplaced foot.

EDNA: But you are mistaken. The saying is 'kick the bucket.'

HILDA: *(Pleased with herself)* It's my eventual death Edna, so if I wish to describe it as such, leave me be. I don't give you metaphors for when Mr Reaper comes a knocking do I?

EDNA: Well played Hilda, well played.

AGATHA coughs.

AGATHA: Oh no, I've got a cough.

HILDA: It will go as soon as it came.

AGATHA coughs again.

AGATHA: There's that dastardly cough again.

EDNA: Nothing to worry about Agatha dear, it's the season for it. Now to the book.

HILDA: Which one shall it be?

HILDA looks through the piles of books on the table.

HILDA: Do we want over or under a hundred-thousand words?

AGATHA coughs again and stands up.

AGATHA: It's the cough.

HILDA stands and checks AGATHA'S temperature.

HILDA: You poor dear, are you quite alright?

AGATHA: I'm not sure; I'm coughing quite a bit.

EDNA watches the exchange and we see her purposely do a cough.

EDNA: Oh, no, me too!

HILDA: What's wrong Edna?

EDNA: I just did a cough.

HILDA: Oh no.

EDNA: I don't believe it; I was right as rain this very morning.

AGATHA and EDNA both cough at each other.

AGATHA: I think that perhaps some of your mint scones would sort out my sudden illness.

EDNA: Yes Doctor Blank prescribes me mint scones when I cough at the surgery.

HILDA: Does he really?

EDNA: Scones!

HILDA: Oh alright, I'll go and see if I have any.

HILDA exits SL. AGATHA and EDNA high-five each other and sit down, rubbing their stomachs.

AGATHA: They are the most heavenly…

EDNA: Minty…

AGATHA / EDNA: Scones!

HILDA enters.

HILDA: The good news is that I have three left.

AGATHA: The bad news?

HILDA: Twenty minutes to defrost.

AGATHA and EDNA both hold their hands over their faces and make sounds. AGATHA stands up suddenly, a massive overreaction to something.

AGATHA: Gosh no!

EDNA / HILDA: What's the matter?

AGATHA: *(Holding up hands)* I've lost my mittens.

HILDA: Have you indeed?

AGATHA: I have and I have, what shall I do?

EDNA: Do without.

AGATHA: Never… I thought my fingers were chilly and I can't possibly turn the pages of a book with frost-bitten digits!

HILDA: Where did you have them last?

AGATHA: This morning at the Tearooms.

HILDA: Ring them on the telephone.

AGATHA: What a good idea.

AGATHA exits SL. HILDA sits down at the table and shakes her head.

HILDA: She's always loosing things; her head would fall off if it wasn't attached in a firm manner.

She notices EDNA looking at her.

HILDA: Please don't say anything to me.

AGATHA enters and sits back at her seat, crumbs on her face.

AGATHA: Any luck?

HILDA and EDNA look at each other.

EDNA: Was there?

AGATHA: Was there what?

EDNA: Any luck?

AGATHA: No answer! I will have to call back again?

HILDA: The phone is in the hall Agatha.

AGATHA: Oh yes, I know that.

HILDA: There isn't a phone in the kitchen.

EDNA: *(Pointing)* SCONES!

HILDA: How could you?

AGATHA: My false teeth are very strong!

EDNA: How impatient, eating mint scones sent from heaven even whilst encrusted in ice!

AGATHA: I'm mighty ashamed as a whole, but my taste buds couldn't give a fuck!

EDNA and HILDA both get up from their seats and back away from AGATHA.

AGATHA: What is wrong with you both?

HILDA: I can't believe you.

AGATHA: I'll bake some more, chill thy beans will you?

HILDA: Not the scones, not my lovely minty scones.

AGATHA: Then what is causing the movements?

EDNA: You said the F word!

AGATHA: I did? Which one?

HILDA: You know very well which one Agatha, and to say it in my house, I really can't look at you right now.

HILDA turns away from her.

EDNA: Give her a moment, she'll come around.

AGATHA: Fudge? Frolic? Feather-bottom? Which one Edna?

EDNA walks to AGATHA and accompanies her to the table.

EDNA: Fuck dear!

AGATHA: Oh, that word is a stranger to me. It hardly ever escapes my inner sanctum.

EDNA: It did just now.

AGATHA: Oh my!

They sit down whilst HILDA rubs her head, confused about something.

AGATHA: Perhaps another visit to the tearooms would act as a locking device? Cream and jam are good clogging devices for words of the devil.

EDNA: Too right we'll visit the tearooms. You can never visit them enough.

AGATHA: Or drink enough tea! I'd happily drown in a gigantic china cup, a digestive as my tombstone, mourners scattering crumbs as my eulogy is shouted.

EDNA: Sounds perfect.

HILDA: He was nearly six feet tall with a ginger beard!

AGATHA: Who was?

EDNA: The husband.

AGATHA: That chestnut.

HILDA returns to the table and picks up the teapot.

HILDA: Tea?

AGATHA / EDNA: Please.

HILDA: Just yesterday I bought some excellent tea leaves enthused with hints of chutney and beef. The market seller said it would make for a very interesting cup.

EDNA: Sounds odd, but I'll give it a go? What was the cup we had last week?

HILDA: That, my dear Edna, was enthused with egg yolk and what they said was 'Super-Weed!' At a guess I'd say it was dandelion.

EDNA: I did enjoy that very much, though at home that evening, I did have trouble saying things. I thought my fridge had teeth and little Timmy Hendrix had a field day come bedtime.

AGATHA: My poor mittens, leaving my naked hands exposed to winter attack!

HILDA: Agatha dear, it is very much August.

AGATHA: I know that but Doctor Blank said I really must assume it's Winter until told otherwise. I am rather cold-blooded to boot.

EDNA: It's old-fashioned is that; people are generally warm-blooded these days.

AGATHA: These days? Pah! How I long for *those* days.

HILDA: Everything *was* much better back then. Last week for example; life was so much better last week than it is today.

AGATHA: A mere seven days can be cruel.

EDNA picks up one of the ruined biscuits.

EDNA: Hilda, do you have any biscuits that haven't been in the wars!

AGATHA: Not like those pesky KitKats! They were around in the war.

HILDA: Were they? *(Stands and shouts SL)* Henry? Were KitKat's around in the war? *(Sits down)* Oh that's right, I live alone.

AGATHA: There…

EDNA: There…

They each pat HILDA on the shoulder nearest to them.

HILDA: My husband!

HILDA plonks her head down on the table and keeps it there. AGATHA stands up, grief-stricken.

AGATHA: My mittens! I've lost both of my mittens, okay?

EDNA stands and pushes her chair gently over.

EDNA: Why can't it be a magazine? There are more pictures than words.

HILDA lifts her head up.

HILDA: I can't even remember what colour his beard was, or if he had a beard at all. Maybe he had no face either? I married only a body… the conversation left a lot to be desired.

AGATHA: How will skin weather the weather?

EDNA: I can't read okay? *(She sighs)* That's right everybody, the secrets out. What use is a book club to a freak like me, somebody tell me that. I need to know, tell me, what use is it?

There is a knock from off-stage. All three women look at each other.

AGATHA: I'm already here!

EDNA: And my arms don't stretch *that* far… anymore.

HILDA: But, who could it be?

KNOCK-KNOCK!

HILDA: *(Standing up)* Who's there?

AGATHA: Hilda, answer the door!

HILDA: I can't answer it, not until I know who is there.

EDNA: Maybe it's your husband.

HILDA: *(Screams at Edna)* He's dead Edna!

EDNA: *(To Agatha)* I thought there was some doubt about that.

KNOCK-KNOCK!

HILDA: I've already asked who is there, and if you cannot be bothered to answer me then I shan't be bothered to open my door.

EDNA: Go away you miserable swine!

AGATHA: Leave us all alone!

MAN'S VOICE: Hilda… Hilda dear?

HILDA stands up and covers her mouth.

HILDA: Is it? It couldn't be could it?

AGATHA: Is it your husband?

HILDA: It could be…

AGATHA: Fantastic news Hilda.

HILDA: Only I have never been married.

HILDA goes off-stage to answer the door.

AGATHA: Let's stop at the tearooms on the way home Edna?

EDNA doesn't move. HILDA returns with a GASMAN.

HILDA: The gasman isn't my husband!

AGATHA: Edna's died I think!

HILDA sits down.

HILDA: Now, which book shall we choose?

Lights down.

For Your Displeasure Plays

Cade Relief and his Butter Feet

Written by Alan Pickthall 2013

Characters

Cade Relief

Annabella

Neil the Narrator

Nasty Chef

Wifey

SCENE ONE

A man walks on the stage, foil wrapped around both of his feet. He has trouble walking and stumbles now and again. He stops centre-stage for a breather, putting his hands on his knees. From off-stage right, we hear a sound of sniffing and imagined tastiness.

CADE RELIEF, whom this fella is by the way, stands straight after wobbling a bit. He goes to run but freezes as NEIL NARRATOR enters dressed dapper and acting confident.

NEIL NARRATOR: Cade Relief and his butter feet, on the run, not to be beaten. For all those who love to eat, best you be quick young butter feet. An accident, a prank? Oh, freak of nature, nurtured in misery, hounded by strangers. Run, quick, Mr Cade Relief, lest some fool eats those butter feet.

NEIL NARRATOR clicks, CADE runs (as best he can) off-stage left.

NEIL NARRATOR: I click because I can, and it makes things quicker. The woman before, ran away too, if she were here I would kick her, because I'm now so busy being Neil the Narrator, and as by the book, back into the shadows… I will see you later.

SCENE TWO

NASTY CHEF, a man in a chef's outfit with a gigantic moustache stands centre-stage, rubbing his belly.

NASTY CHEF: Nom-nom, Yum-yum, a storm's a brewing inside me tum! I need a fix of something filling, a recipe all delicious like melting trotters, even if the ingredient itself is unwilling.

WIFEY (his wife) enters; a big dress with a daft head.

WIFEY: Oh, Nasty Chef, my husband dear, what on earth is that earthquake I hear? Please do tell me, it's not that belly, which shakes our walls, makes the room smelly?

NASTY CHEF: I'm so very afraid that the sounds that I make can never be dulled until I spread from a leg, a flavour so yummy, it fills me tummy more than the sweetest of cakes. For all over the papers, something that takes us and gets our minds whirling, guts knotted and churning – a human being with feet of butter, a flavour I'm sure unlike any other.

WIFEY: You are a Nasty Chef, but the cupboards are bare. There's nothing left. There's been a recession and much more I am guessing. To cut a knob from a toe would overthrow your hunger and bring us together, we could live happily ever after, *(Holds up a newspaper)* I have seen the paper! Wanted is he, but not for a crime, in a pan is this boy bound, not the 'usual' doing of time. I support you, I'm with you, go get your net. You'll be the greatest chef England has seen yet.

NASTY CHEF grabs his WIFEY's hands, looking into her eyes.

NASTY CHEF: Thank you Wifey, I owe you my life, a good wife such as you. Let us go together and find the one that will make me famous, leave us a taste of youth. I've a glorious feeling and the cows that go 'moo,' will make my business receive words of good favour, a five-star review. Go and grab your torch Wifey, please, as soon it be night-time, and Nom-nom, Yum-yum, a storm's a brewing deep down in me tum.

SCENE THREE

CADE RELIEF stumbles on-stage, falling to the floor. He turns over on to his back and leans up, using his elbows followed by hands for support.

CADE: *(Panting)* Miles and hours I've come through thick fog, I'm tired, I'm aching, not only that but good God, I hear voices and sounds of deep, gurgling guts. Shouldn't lie down for too long or my feet are kaput!

He moves around with his hands, feet never touching the floor, till he ends on his knees. CADE clasps his hands together.

CADE: You know I am not a religious man, but whatever's out there, I believe that you can, guide me and hide me, increase my lifespan. It's been just over a year and three months since I first ran. It wasn't my fault, I'm like this, and it's who I am. How ironic that all dairy makes me sick, I'm allergic, never have I been a fan!

ANNABELLA enters SR, sees CADE in his knees.

ANNABELLA: *(to herself)* Look at you there, fake-praying on your knees. Oh I love you Cade Relief, I see over the two parts everyone sees. It makes me so sad to think there are worse folk out to taste those wonders on the end of both foot-sticks, that I only hope we make haste an escape to a place so cool, you'll always walk for oneself. We could live and be happy, no need for friends or jobs and wealth. A white picket fence, one that sparkles like no other, let's hope our children's feet are spared the fate of being pure butter. *(She moves toward him)* Cade!

CADE: Annabella!

She leans down and hugs him.

ANNABELLA: I've missed you so much. It's been weeks since that we spoke; I have been 'busy' as such.

CADE: No need to worry about that because there's bigger fish to fry, I've avoided some close calls and I'll now tell you why...

They speak, but silently, moving mouths to form shapes that could never really be words.

NEIL NARRATOR enters.

NEIL NARRATOR: Back, did you miss me? Neil Narrator I am, in case you weren't listening! Cade and Annabella, two friends, possible lovers speak silently; don't know about you, but me? Their mouths move, forming shapes that could never be used, maybe to throw off scents, making sure that they cannot be heard.

CADE: What's that?

NEIL NARRATOR: Cade says, his eyes deep, panicked pools.

ANNABELLA: What do you hear?

NEIL NARRATOR: Annabella, clears her throat, she heard it too... They turn their heads in the direction of a hungry tune. A song from over there, where the dark lives, footsteps approaching in the fog, two shapes and what looks like a big sieve, but it's not...

CADE: A net!

ANNABELLA: Get up Cade, stand up.

CADE: I can't, I need water, I'm too tired, body and mind. I ought to; I see that but this may be it.

ANNABELLA tries to pull him to his feet, reaching under his arms. He is a deadweight.

NEIL NARRATOR: Could this be where our, admittedly short, tale ends? A censored love story of two more of those 'could be more than friends?' Cade and Annabella, struggle to make an exit.

NASTY CHEF and WIFEY enter SR, he holds a big net, she dangles a loaf of bread from a hand.

NASTY CHEF: Nasty Chef!

WIFEY: And Wifey!

NEIL NARRATOR: No need to announce it! But that is who they are and as a narrator, all I can do is to watch what happens without interference, much the same as you all are doing.

NEIL NARRATOR leaves the stage and sits with the audience, taking out a bag of popcorn and eating some, offering the audience a taste.

NEIL NARRATOR: The popcorn is buttered, please don't judge me.

ANNABELLA: You, both of you, stay well away.

NASTY CHEF: My dear, I'm soon to become a famous chef. I'm a nasty so and so and so, cooking is all I have left.

WIFEY: An ingredient nobody else had will put my husband on the map, so perhaps you should move from out of his way. This probably won't hurt, a quick slice and it's done, and there will be no waste. I've even brought a loaf of doughy fine bread, for a sneaky little taste.

CADE: Why don't you just leave me alone? You've butter in your fridge, so use that that instead. What difference would my butter feet make, except kill me dead? I've tried hard to keep them a certain temperature for all of these years, yet you would spoil all my efforts with some bread, that isn't fair, it would bring me to tears.

NEIL NARRATOR: Cade said!

NASTY CHEF: Dearest Wifey, my little dear wife… if you would be so kind as to rid this scene of the girl, I've a feeling she'll be a nuisance. My brain's already in a whirl of excitement, can't wait for a slice of buttery goodness from my good man sat right here.

WIFEY: I hear you, I'm on it, throw me the net, idiot husband of mine…

He does give her the net.

WIFEY: And I'll teach this silly girl a lesson, not to stand in the way of fine dining.

CADE: Run Annabella!

WIFEY puts the net over her head before she can run.

ANNABELLA: Too late, I am caught. So sorry Cade but let it be known that I've loved you forever, just thought that I'd say.

WIFEY: Hush!

NASTY CHEF looks on as CADE attempts to help ANNABELLA but fails, falling to the floor.

CADE: Anyway, I've always known it, hip, hip hooray and the rest of that. Such a shame to be only sat, not able to save a damsel whom I so love, I guess it's another teenage tragedy, two flowers in bloom, but these flowers are doomed, so it wasn't meant to be.

NASTY CHEF sits down next to CADE, speaking into his ear.

NASTY CHEF: You see? It's for the best that I get the best from feet so sweet; I can whiff them from here. Sit back, relax and let me unwrap, what will make me God or at the very least a slap on the thigh tasty Chef.

NEIL NARRATOR: Don't forget nasty!

NASTY CHEF looks at WIFEY

WIFEY: Look not at my face, it said nothing.

NASTY CHEF: No matter, that I am, that's why I'm unwrapping *(slowly unwraps the left-foot foil),* the left foot foil, to discover the butter that will make my sole a most delectable dish, one astonishing fish that critics will adore.

ANNABELLA: I can't watch.

WIFEY: Won't hurt.

CADE: Biting lip.

NASTY CHEF slices some butter from the foot and tastes it on the bread from WIFEY.

NASTY CHEF: That's it, I'm done.

CADE: He's done?

ANNABELLA: So he says, spread the butter on bread, not a granary bun. Did it hurt?

CADE: Not a bit.

NASTY CHEF: *(Holding mouth)* Owww!

WIFEY: What's wrong?

NASTY CHEF: My lip has grown big!

ANNABELLA / CADE: He must be allergic!

They look at each other.

ANNABELLA / CADE: That's what I said!

WIFEY let's go of ANNABELLA and runs to comfort NASTY CHEF.

WIFEY: You two will be sorry if he ends up dead.

ANNABELLA: Well, that's what you get.

CADE: Yes, you deserve what you get.

NEIL NARRATOR clicks his fingers from the audience and stands up; the rest of the cast freeze. He stands up and walks into the scene.

NEIL NARRATOR: Yes, indeed what you get, you'll end up dead when you try and steal, butter from feet and wipe it on bread. I've been your Neil Narrator and I'm signing off… shame nobody told Nasty Chef that Cade Relief's butter feet were off too, so toodle-oo, and adieu.

NEIL NARRATOR clicks and the lights go to BLACKOUT.

THE END OF IT

Clyde² = Auntie Lydia

Written by Alan Pickthall 2010

Characters

Rich

Mitch

Dick

Clyde

THE 1ST SCENE

Three men on-stage, front-centre; RICH, MITCH and DICK – they are dressed up for a night on the town.

RICH: This taxi is taking the piss.

MITCH: When did you call it?

RICH: Yesterday.

MITCH: Really? Yesterday?

DICK: Why do that?

RICH: Dick, if I'd left it to you we wouldn't be having a night out. We'd be stuck in your bedroom.

DICK: What's wrong with my bedroom?

RICH: What's right with it?

MITCH: It's got a dead funny smell, there's 'happy' tissues everywhere…

RICH: You're a chronic fiddler.

DICK: I have nasal trouble, it's *serious*.

MITCH: And there are bits of old food in the curtains… and the drawers.

DICK: The doctor said it was serious. I'm inclined to believe him; he's a doctor.

RICH: Which one was it? The serious doctor or the funny one?

MITCH: Yep, Dr Stern or Dr Smiley?

DICK: Dr Blank.

RICH and MITCH both laugh.

RICH: Who else!

MITCH: Of course it would be Dr Blank – has this world no other doctors?

RICH: You do know he was arrested for murder not so long ago; he's a lunatic, my mum even said as much.

DICK: Allegations at the moment lads, nothing proven yet.

RICH: Dr Blank my arse. I'm still glad we didn't end up in your bedroom. Or as I have since renamed it, 'The Emporium of Stains.'

DICK: Where's Clyde?

RICH: A subject change I see.

DICK: Mitch, will you give Clyde a ring.

MITCH: Marry him yourself you coward.

DICK: Good one, well done; will you give him a call?

MITCH: I already have.

DICK: When?

MITCH: Just now.

DICK: *Just* now, while we've been stood here?

MITCH: That's right, I'm lightning fast with the old mobile, network is a dream.

DICK: That can't be.

MITCH / RICH: *(Mimicking Dick)* That can't be!

RICH: He's pulling your foot-sticks you dick.

DICK: May I remind you, 'dick' isn't the greatest of put-downs, since my name actually is Dick.

RICH looks at MITCH and turns back to DICK.

RICH: Okay then… twat!

DICK: That's better. You'd do well to remember that for future reference.

RICH: I could fill a book with names I could call you.

DICK: That so is it?

RICH: So-err than so.

MITCH: Would you like me to call him and see where he is? For real this time.

DICK: Thanks Mitch that would be wonderful. And Rich, up yours!

RICH: Yours would be a pamphlet.

MITCH types numbers into his mobile while the others watch him.

MITCH: It's ringing.

RICH: Wow technology is ace.

DICK: He does know about tonight, I remember telling him.

MITCH: Still ringing, come on Clyde, answer the phone.

RICH: I haven't seen him for weeks.

MITCH: Answer phone.

RICH: I did accuse him of fancying pigeons, maybe that's why!

MITCH: 'Hi Clyde, it's Mitch, how you doing buddy? Me, Rich and Dick are just wondering where you are – it's Debbie's birthday tonight. Dick says he did tell you…'

DICK: I *did*, I did tell you.

RICH: Shush Dick.

MITCH: 'He swears on it in fact. But if for some reason he didn't or you've forgotten, get yourself over to mine now. A taxi should be here in the next ten. It'd be nice to have all four of us together again. Give me a call when you get this message and I'll tell you where we are.'

DICK: Tell him he needs to bring that tenner he owes me.

RICH: And remind him he jacks off in parks.

DICK hits RICH in the arm.

RICH: Because of the pigeons, not because he's a pervert or anything.

MITCH: 'Right, well I'm guessing you heard all of that so, we'll see you soon mate, bye.'

MITCH ends the call and puts the phone back into his pocket.

RICH: Is he coming?

MITCH: I've just realised Rich, that you're an amazingly funny person. If I were you, I'd go stick a hand on that wall over there and walk back repeatedly into it.

RICH: Tell you what dude; you've a clever, clever brain there. I think you should make it cleverer and go eat Einstein.

DICK: You can't eat Einstein. You're not funny either.

RICH: I bet Mitch could, couldn't you Mitch? Pop him on a plate, dash of Tommy K, and chow on down, see where that gets you!

MITCH: Kiss my internals.

RICH taps him on the stomach.

RICH: Go on then, get them out!

DICK: Tonight's going to be fun.

RICH: I bet I could kick your arse.

MITCH: I bet I'd be too fast for you. Your heart would go on holiday before you caught me.

MITCH and RICH square up to each other, RICH turns to DICK.

RICH: He's being all clever again.

RICH jumps on MITCH and they scuffle for a bit. DICK spots something where the audience are and begins pointing.

DICK: Police car!

The scuffle stops and all three lads stand normally, hands in pockets, whistling – RICH waves and DICK smiles. They watch the car go by.

MITCH: Want some more?

RICH: I've got two fists to cave your skull in matey.

MITCH: Don't call me matey, mate.

RICH: Dick, lend him a word will you?

DICK: *(Bored)* Tosser.

RICH: Yeah that's what you are.

MITCH: And you… you're an absolute, *fiend!*

They all go silent, briefly gazing at each other. They then begin to laugh stupidly.

RICH: That's a good one that.

DICK: An absolute keeper.

MITCH: Absolute fiend is what I said.

All three sigh – silence for 5 seconds.

RICH: We have a laugh don't we?

MITCH: Course we do, we're the best ever.

DICK: At doing what?

MITCH: Having a laugh.

DICK: Right, wish Clyde was here though. He likes a laugh he does.

RICH: *(Pointing towards audience)* Here's the taxi.

Lights fade down.

THE 2nd SCENE

CLYDE enters, holding a Dictaphone and speaking into it.

CLYDE: None the wiser; my research thus far has come to nothing. I did find out that smiles are just wilful spasms and that drinking tears gives you another ten years. Nothing more though, the progression is very slow and I remain without clue. My Auntie has been dead for twenty years now, the recipe, still secret.

He takes out a notepad and pen from his pocket and places the Dictaphone under an arm. He writes the following down...

CLYDE: *(Slow)* Find... out... secret.

He returns the notebook and pen, resuming his speech back into the Dictaphone.

CLYDE: I'm still unsure if resurrecting the deceased is ethical, is it the *right* thing to do? In this instance I'd say it is, undeniably so. Too risky to not do anything and not doing nothing isn't an option. I've seen many a film with various depictions of resurrection, some seem far-fetched and implausible. There are actions and ideas that I have noted and will be trying, but alas, still short of a breakthrough. All I wish is that my determination and damn stupidity will provide a platform for success and that nothing happens to me whilst I search for the means. If I died, would somebody bother to bring me back to breathing? Would anyone notice I was even gone? *(Pause)* I feel a bit upset now.

Lights fade down.

THE 3rd SCENE

RICH, MITCH and DICK all stand stage-left, holding a drink each. Quiet, classical music plays in the background.

MITCH: Is this the right place? I don't see anyone we know.

DICK: Debbie's not one for 'too loud', I think she might be running late.

MITCH: What about her family though? They'd be here since it's her birthday and I see none of them.

RICH: Have you ever met any of her family?

MITCH: *(Shouts)* No.

DICK: There you are then; any of these could be her family. All of them even.

RICH: What about that guy over there?

DICK: Dad.

RICH: And that short lass over there with the spikey eye?

DICK: Sister?

MITCH: *(Shakes head)* Wrong place, it's obvious.

DICK: Let's go somewhere else.

RICH: Let's go to that other club, the one over there.

RICH points to the other side of the stage.

MITCH: Yeah, nice one.

All three walk over to the other side of the stage – the music changes from classical to thrash-punk. They are 'in another club now!'

DICK: Doesn't seem very 'Debbie' to me.

MITCH: Define Debbie.

DICK: I don't know; I just don't think this club would sleep with just anyone.

MITCH: I guess, I'm not going to be able to enjoy myself here.

RICH has been moshing with other public pogo-ers, he turns to the two stood still.

RICH: Come on now straight laces have a jig!

MITCH: Okay but just a small one.

All three mosh for a moment or two. MITCH hurts his neck and has to stop. The other two soon follow.

MITCH: Bloody hell, I'm not that young anymore.

RICH: You're 18!

MITCH: Not as young as I was though.

DICK: Everyone's never as young as they were. I'm older than I was when I first started this sentence.

RICH: And I'm older than I was when he finished it… and now.

MITCH: Point taken.

RICH: Come on; let's try that other close-by bar.

RICH points to the centre-stage front. They all walk over to it, still with the same drinks. They look around the new surroundings.

DICK: This is the place.

RICH: You sure?

DICK: Look there, 'Happy Birthday Debbie' banners, all around the place.

RICH: That could be any old Debbie. There's more than one Debbie in the world.

MITCH: *(Looking forward)* There's Debbie there.

RICH: Where?

MITCH: Right there.

RICH looks, sees Debbie, who we don't see and must imagine her side of the conversation. RICH waves and shouts over.

RICH: Oi, Debbie! Debbie, over here…

DICK: Is she ignoring us, she is, isn't she? She's totally ignorant.

MITCH: *(To Rich)* You haven't accused *her* of fancying pigeons have you?

RICH: No. I don't think so.

DICK: She's seen us – she's on her way over, quick guys, act cool-tastic.

All three smarten themselves, checking hair and flexing imaginary muscles.

DICK: Hi.

RICH pushes DICK out of the way, smiling.

RICH: Hi Debbie, Happy Birthday… don't worry, of course… we wouldn't miss it… no, Clyde's not with us…

MITCH: You look great… thanks, I don't exercise, don't know what that is… I always thought that… chips probably…

DICK: So Debbie…

DICK is again pushed out of the way by RICH.

RICH: Let me buy you a birthday drink… or drinks… your call…

DICK taps RICH on the shoulder.

DICK: Excuse me Rich.

RICH: Yes *Dick? (turns to Debbie)* His name!

DICK: It seems like you keep interup…

RICH: Three triple vodkas it is… gosh I know, it's like nine vodkas…

DICK: Stop interrupting me, let me speak.

RICH: You are speaking.

DICK: To Debbie.

RICH: To Debbie?

DICK: Debbie, Debbie, Debbie!

RICH: You don't have to say Debbie three times; it won't make me three times more bothered.

MITCH: She's gone! Well done dunces, she's gone to wag chins with crack-head over there.

RICH: I knew I should have said yes when I was a kid.

LIGHTS FADE DOWN

THE 4TH SCENE

CLYDE has an old torn box which he sifts through; he sits next to it. 'Lydia's Earthly Possessions' is written on the side of it.

CLYDE: Come on, where is it? It must be here somewhere.

He pulls out a pair of glasses which he puts on and a scarf which he sniffs.

CLYDE: Nothing left on it; not that I can smell.

He carries on rummaging and pulls out a hairbrush.

CLYDE: That's what I'm after. Yes, there's plenty on it.

He carefully pulls a hair off the brush. He has a jar next to him. He slowly opens the lid and places the hair inside.

CLYDE: I'm halfway there.

He pulls a handkerchief from the box, studies it and puts it into the jar.

CLYDE: I'll get the recipe, no doubt, I knew I would. I'm either a genius or a genuine arse.

He takes a knife out of his pocket and turns his back to the audience. We hear a yelp come from him.

CLYDE: This better be worth it.

He turns around; we see he has bled into the jar. He takes the Dictaphone from his pocket and speaks into it.

CLYDE: To sum up at this point… I have bled into the jar containing Lydia's snot-rag and single hair. No reaction at the moment. Maybe I'm expecting too much in such a short space of time. It may have to be injected into the corpse for it to take effect.

Note to self – borrow mum's shovel and a pair of rubber gloves, not the special ones though *(pause)* and get her to bake me a cake, chocolate.

He turns off the Dictaphone.

CLYDE: Some of me, some of her. I'll need another extract of Clyde, yep, stupid third person Clyde. I *am* Clyde.

He holds his face and pulls one cheek outwards.

CLYDE: Still me!

His mobile phone rings.

CLYDE: Don't answer it; you'll never get into those jeans if you do. It could be important. See if I care, answer it if you want to. It'll be your dickhead friends wondering where you are. You've a dozen missed calls already, what's the harm in another? But if I don't answer it they might cut the ties of friendship, I'll end up a lonely old man – a Mr Spinster with a bloody jar. Don't say I didn't warn you Clyde. Okay Clyde, thanks for the input.

He answers the phone.

CLYDE: Hi Mitch.

MITCH appears on the opposite side of the stage – RICH and DICK dance in the background. Whenever MITCH talks the music blares loudly, whenever CLYDE talks, it disappears almost completely.

MITCH: So you can answer a phone you gonk? Where are you?

CLYDE: I'm at home Mitch.

MITCH: At home! *(He tells the others)* He's still at home *(they shrug and keep dancing)* Why don't you come?

CLYDE: I'm pretty busy to be honest.

MITCH: Doing what?

CLYDE: *(To himself)* Think of something fast, what could I have been doing that doesn't sound like a lie?

MITCH: You do know I can hear you Clyde?

CLYDE: Sorry, I thought that was internal.

MITCH: Here… now! All the boys are here, all three of us, and Debbie's here. She's been asking for you.

CLYDE: Debbie's there?

MITCH: It's her birthday, she's here alright.

CLYDE: Debbie, she's the reason I'm doing this.

MITCH: The reason you're doing what?

CLYDE: Erm…

MITCH: Seriously Clyde, thoughts are for inside.

CLYDE: Sorry, how does she look?

MITCH: Debbie?

CLYDE: What's she wearing? Describe her for me.

MITCH: You've got both hands occupied above the waist haven't you?

CLYDE: It's not like that. I just want to know if she looks beautiful tonight, that's all.

MITCH looks around at 'Debbie'.

MITCH: A dress, it's green – she looks fit okay?

CLYDE: Only the best Yorkshire puddings for Debbie.

MITCH: What was that?

CLYDE: Apologise to her for me, but I'm staying in for her.

MITCH: Are you trying to make her heart grow fonder or what?

CLYDE: Something like that.

CLYDE ends the call – MITCH looks at the phone, annoyed, and puts it back in his pocket. He starts dancing with RICH and DICK and they dance off-stage.

CLYDE: Now, gotta think about another component for the jar mix. It must be something of mine.

He crosses his legs together.

CLYDE: Right after I've had a piss.

He stops and thinks.

CLYDE: Maybe that's it.

He waddles off-stage with the jar in both trembling hands.

LIGHTS FADE DOWN.

THE 5TH SCENE

RICH is hunched over with his back to the audience. MITCH and DICK stand either side of him, patting his back. RICH makes massive retching sounds, trying to vomit.

MITCH: That's it mate, get it all up, better out than in, like farts, but from your mouth.

DICK: Certainly smells the same. Know your limit is all I'll say.

MITCH: That's really no help.

DICK: Drink responsibly.

MITCH: Shut up mate.

DICK: Right you are *(he looks over Rich)* yum, look at all those chunks. It's bizarre, where did they come from?

RICH vomits again.

MITCH: His sick's making me sick.

DICK: It doesn't bother me sick, I could eat the stuff.

MITCH: Could you?

DICK: If I had something pointing towards my head.

MITCH points a finger towards DICK and then to the sick.

DICK: I was thinking a gun Mitch.

MITCH pulls out a gun and points it at DICK. DICK leaves RICH and steps back with his hands up in surrender.

DICK: Where the hell did you get that?

MITCH: For Christmas! It's not loaded; I just carry it around to look hard.

DICK: Put it away.

MITCH: Fine.

MITCH puts it away.

DICK: Thank you.

MITCH: Dick, I'm worried about Clyde.

DICK: Did you talk to him?

MITCH: I did, he said he was staying in *for* Debbie.

DICK: That's odd.

MITCH: That's right, and he was all talking like I wasn't listening… mentioned Yorkshire puddings too.

DICK: *(Serious)* Good Lord.

MITCH: What's wrong?

DICK: Not sure really. Clyde's been trying to sleep with Debbie for about two years now.

MITCH: And?

DICK: Well you know how much Debbie wants to be a chef right?

MITCH: I am familiar with that dream.

RICH steps forward.

RICH: Familiar with what?

MITCH: The dream.

RICH: Debbie's yeah, hey, how about we give her the bumps?

DICK: She's nineteen.

RICH: Exactly, we could knock her the fuck out.

DICK: And that would be fun for you?

RICH: *(Shrugs)* Maybe not *fun* fun, but fun-ny? Yes! It will be something to tell the grandchildren.

MITCH: Mmm 'come and sit on my knee and let me tell you how I fractured the skull of a friend of mine' – I'm sure they'd be riveted.

RICH: It beats 'oh, I eat a pasty when I was twelve!'

DICK: I think we should try and enjoy the rest of the night and go see Clyde at the weekend.

MITCH: Supposes.

RICH: What are we worrying about him for anyway? He didn't bother to come so let's forget him and start pulling.

MITCH: There's not much to pull. Everyone in here's either sixty or not even born.

RICH: A few greys never stopped me.

MITCH: Don't we know it!

DICK: Yes Rich please stop posting photographs on my *Facebook*.

RICH: Well, we're all grave-bound so let's live a little while we can.

MITCH: *(Pause)* Bit cheesy but all right.

RICH: Point me a target.

MITCH and DICK both point toward somebody.

MITCH / DICK: Her!

RICH: Fair enough, you two follow my lead; we'll see who she chooses. That guy *(coughs)* me, gets his drinks bought the rest of the night. Kapushnicov?

MITCH / DICK: Kapushnicov.

Music

All three lads pull collars up, sniff armpits and adjust crotches in unison. DICK and MITCH pat RICH on the shoulder to go first. Rich struts over to a woman we cannot see, he leans over and makes a sexual gesture with his hands. She is offended by this and Rich walks back to the shaking heads of his friends.
Mitch walks over next and pulls a deck of cards from his pocket. He holds the cards out and she takes one; as he shuffles the cards, he drops them all over the floor. She turns her back while he is on all fours; he looks up, notices this, gathers the cards together and walks back to the friends who are bursting with laughter.
Dick walks over next – as he approaches, the woman walks away, his head follows her in disappointment. He walks back to the others who have put their hands over faces.
They quickly discuss something and point in the woman's direction, following her off-stage.

CLYDE enters the opposite side holding the jar that now contains blood, piss, a hair and a tissue all bloody mixed together. He holds it up and studies it, looking like a mad scientist. He takes the top off of the jar and gulps some down. He waits, a sudden pain in his stomach – he puts the jar down – and falls on all fours to the floor. He lifts his head up, wide-eyed and pulls a lipstick out from his pocket... as he stands he puts it on his lips and leaves a trail that rises up to his temple. He laughs and pulls out a pen and paper from his pocket. He begins to scribble furiously before walking off oddly where he entered.

RICH, MITCH and DICK re-enter, holding noses and necks; they've been in a fight of some kind.

Music fades.

DICK: Who's buying the drinks then?

MITCH: I don't think anyone won, Rich?

RICH: Mitch?

MITCH: No Dick, nobody won!

DICK: Never mind, there's always licky bum-bum.

RICH and MITCH look at him.

DICK: You didn't hear that.

MITCH: I think I'm off.

RICH: I'm riper than ever; it's only half past midnight.

MITCH: They'll be shutting down soon.

DICK: You wanna go and see Clyde don't you?

MITCH: There's something a tad wrong with the sitch.

RICH: Your infatuation with Clyde is a tad wrong – he may as well have actually been here! 'I must ring Clyde, oh gosh; Clyde's making Yorkshire's' bloody Clyde.

MITCH: Sometimes I really don't like you, you know that?

RICH: I do now. And my minds mutual.

MITCH: Your mind is mutual?

RICH: That's right, mutual minds.

He points back and forth between his head and MITCH's.

DICK: Let's *all* go, it's on the way and once we know he's not gone sour, we'll all have mutual minds, if I think what you mean is what you actually mean.

RICH: What do you mean?

MITCH: Thank you Dick-chard; the voice of reason undoubtedly.

RICH: You mean the voice of...

RICH lifts his leg and farts.

MITCH: Well I'm happy there was an appropriate context for your party trick for once.

DICK: I'll pat you on the back in the back of the taxi, let's flag one down.

RICH: When you say that I just imagine us with three poles, bashing down on the bonnet until he agrees to a free drop off!

MITCH: Let's say bye to Debbie first.

RICH: And warn her about Clyde.

MITCH: I don't think we should mention that just yet, he's probably just having an off day.

DICK: He'll be fine.

RICH: I'm going to have to visit the men's first, I think I may have laid some turf in my under crackers.

All three walk off – RICH walking and holding the seat of his trousers outwards.

Lights down.

THE 6TH SCENE

CLYDE walks on with oven gloves, holding a tray of Yorkshire puddings. He is still wearing the lipstick and also has Auntie Lydia's jewellery and scarf on his person.

CLYDE: *(Sniffs puddings)* Risen to perfection, these have to be the best flipping Yorkshire's in… Yorkshire… or the world perhaps!
(Adopts Auntie Lydia's voice) I did make the best, how tragic I died so young – depriving my loved ones of the beautiful culinary skills I possessed.
(Clyde) Too right Auntie Lydia, but I've got it now; I can spread the word, like a good, happy, disease.
(Lydia) Go ahead and tuck in my boy. Fill your boots, so they say.
(Clyde) I couldn't, got to save them for Debbie. She's going to take one bite of these and shag me senseless. So much so I'll have to get some kind of sex swing installed in the kitchen so I can bake and make love at the very same time.
(Pause)
(Lydia) What was that?
(Clyde) You heard.
(Lydia) I wouldn't have a relative of mine use my recipe for such sordid reasons.
(Clyde) It's not sordid Auntie Lydia, just natural humanistics!
(Lydia) Bullshit; give me them back.

CLYDE should now act like each arm is one of the two different people inhabiting his body; himself and AUNTIE LYDIA. There is now a tug of war with the baking tray.

CLYDE: No, I'm keeping them thank you very much.
(Lydia) Hand them over Clyde, or I'll tell your mother.
(Clyde) Tell her, she never liked you anyway.
(Lydia) Here!
(Clyde) I'll just bake more.

The result of the battle is that the Yorkshire puddings fly off the tray and scatter all over the floor.

CLYDE: You bitch…
(Lydia) Where's the recipe?
(Clyde) In my pocket… damn it.

He/she pulls the recipe out of his pocket, another tug of war occurs. Lydia's side raises the paper above his head and Clyde tries to grab at it with his hand.

CLYDE: *(As Lydia)* We need to rip it.
(Clyde) No don't, let's talk.
(Lydia) Too late.

He/she uses both hands (one reluctantly) and rips the recipe in two.

CLYDE: *(Raised voice)* How could I be so stupid?
(Lydia) Very easily – hey, you know what?
(Clyde) What?

Lydia's hand punches him in the balls – CLYDE falls over.

CLYDE: What did you do that for?
(Lydia) I've just always wanted to do it, never got the chance… hurt did it?
(Clyde) Yes.
(Lydia) Good.

There is a knock from off-stage and we hear voices.

MITCH: Clyde?

CLYDE: Oh no, Mitch.

MITCH: It's us.

DICK: Your mates.

RICH: Yeah, open up or I'm shitting on your doorstep.

CLYDE: I'd really rather you all just went.

MITCH: Open the door.

CLYDE: *(As Lydia)* Destroy them all!
(Clyde) I will not.

MITCH: Is someone in there with you?

CLYDE: *(As Lydia)* Yes, now go and bugger yourself.
(Clyde) No… just me.

RICH: You saucy minx, have you got a lass in there or what?

CLYDE: No, it's my Auntie Lydia.

RICH: Err, you wrong bastard.

CLYDE: Not like that.

DICK: The doors open, just go in.

CLYDE: No.
(Lydia) Yes.
(Clyde) No.
(Lydia) Yes.

MITCH, RITCH and DICK enter and see CLYDE having an arm wrestle with himself.

MITCH: What's happening?

DICK: That's what I want to know.

CLYDE: The spirit of my dead Auntie Lydia's inside of me; I squared myself.

DICK / RICH / MITCH: Eh?

CLYDE: I needed the recipe to woo Debbie.

RICH: Is that some kind of sexy act I haven't heard before?

DICK: No.

MITCH: Yes *(to Dick)* It's quicker!

RICH: Cool as silk.

CLYDE: Trouble is, she's being a bit of a knob.
(Lydia) I am not.
(Clyde) Yeah right.

MITCH: What can we do?

CLYDE: I think somebody is going to have to knock me out. Get her out.

RICH: *(Hand up)* I'll do it.

MITCH: You sure Clyde?

CLYDE: *(as Lydia)* Nope.

RICH: *(Disappointed)* Man.

CLYDE: Yes.

RICH: *(Excited)* Come on.

CLYDE: Do it now.

RICH walks over to CLYDE and begins to beat him up.

DICK: Rich? I think you need to just knock him on the head.

RICH, who is giving CLYDE a kick in the shin, turns around.

RICH: All in good time Dick.

He returns to CLYDE and begins punching him in the stomach.

RICH: Get out of him you whore.

CLYDE: *(Between punches)* That's... my... Auntie... you're talking about.

DICK: *(to Mitch)* Doesn't this all seem a bit far-fetched?

MITCH: *(to Dick)* Go with it.

RICH: That's it Grot-bags; leave my friend alone.

CLYDE: *(Between punches)* Don't... speak... ill... of... the dead.

CLYDE falls to the floor unconscious and RICH keeps hitting him.

MITCH: Rich?

DICK: Richard?

RICH looks up.

MITCH: I think he's out cold.

RICH looks at CLYDE who is motionless on the floor.

RICH: Yeah he looks it.

MITCH and DICK join RICH and stand over CLYDE's body.

DICK: Poor sod.

MITCH: He's had it tough these past few years, tougher than most.

RICH: It looks like he's sleeping, dreaming of fists, little blighter.

DICK: Let's sing a song in remembrance.

MITCH: He's not dead.

DICK: Let's sing one anyway.

MITCH: Let's not.

RICH: I'm glad this situation presented itself. I've always wanted to hurt and protect him in equal measure.

MITCH: Well done.

RICH: Thanks.

DICK: I can see why he did it like; Debbie is pretty, *pretty,* hot.

MITCH: She is.

RICH: I've dreamt of her naked once or twice.

MITCH and DICK think about this.

MITCH / DICK: Me too!

RICH: Maybe she isn't worth going insane for.

MITCH: Not sure about that Rich. She's the coolest girl in the world.

DICK: Quite a catch.

RICH: I'm in total love with her.

MITCH: *You're* in love with Debbie.

RICH: That's what I said.

MITCH: I'm going to ask her out.

DICK: Not before I do.

RICH: I can see myself marrying her.

MITCH: I can see myself marrying her, divorcing her after a few years and having massive make-up bosh once we realize that after another decade that we should have never split up in the first place.

DICK: Got it all figured out have you?

MITCH reaches down and picks up a Yorkshire pudding.

MITCH: My life's going to be wicked.

RICH picks up another pudding.

RICH: Debbie and Rich sitting in a tree…

DICK picks up, yes, you guessed it… a massive house… no, kidding, another Yorkshire pudding.

DICK: We're going to have ten kids me and Debbs!

All three lads start eyeing each other up.

MITCH: Debbs now is it? I'm telling you both, she's mine.

DICK: Not a chance.

RICH: Not with me in the picture anyway.

DICK: Dick and Debbie, it's a given.

MITCH: We can't all have her. Clyde's out of the running but we've got to come to an agreement.

DICK: You're right.

RICH: There's only one way to find out…

MITCH / RICH / DICK: FIGHT!

All three fight in slow motion to some lovely music.

As they do so, CLYDE begins to stir and eventually sits up looking at his friends brawling.

Yorkshires are thrown and used as gags. Punches and kicks are thrown.

Music stops and the three carry on fighting, but in real-time.

CLYDE shakes his head and speaks in Auntie Lydia's voice.

CLYDE: *(As Lydia)* I was never very good at Maths…

Music comes on again and the fight continues.

CLYDE eats a Yorkshire pudding as he watches from the floor.

LIGHTS DOWN.

ABOUT THE AUTHOR

Alan Pickthall is a Performing Arts lecturer in the North East of England. He has written over 25 plays and is currently finishing his novel, *HIS EVIL STAR*, to be published later in 2015, along with further volumes of *For Your Displeasure Plays.* Find him on *Facebook* and *Twitter*.

Printed in Great Britain
by Amazon.co.uk, Ltd.,
Marston Gate.